Stockton -
    LIBR

Stockton & Billingham C

T017222

KU-514-465

4339501003098442772b012

30895

STUDIES IN ENGLISH LITERATURE No. 58

General Editor

David Daiches

Professor of English in the School of English
and American Studies, University of Sussex

Already published in the series:

SHAKESPEARE: CORIOLANUS

by
BRIAN VICKERS

Professor of English and Renaissance
Literature, ETH, Zürich

EDWARD ARNOLD

© BRIAN VICKERS 1976

First published 1976
by Edward Arnold (Publishers) Ltd,
25 Hill Street, London W1X 8LL

Cloth edition: ISBN 0 7131 5847 6
Paper edition: ISBN 0 7131 5860 3

All Rights Reserved. No part of this publication may be reproduced,
stored in a retrieval system, or transmitted, in any form or by any means,
electronic, mechanical, photocopying, recording or otherwise, without
the prior permission of Edward Arnold (Publishers) Ltd.

This book is published in two editions. The paperback edition is sold
subject to the condition that it shall not by way of trade or otherwise, be
lent, resold, hired out, or otherwise circulated without the publisher's
prior consent in any form of binding or cover other than that in which it
is published and without a similar condition including this condition
being imposed on the subsequent purchaser.

Stockton - Billingham
LIBRARY
Technical College

To the students, teachers and staff of the
Englisches Seminar, University of Zürich

822 SHA

30895

Printed in Great Britain by
The Camelot Press Ltd, Southampton

General Preface

The object of this series is to provide studies of individual novels, plays and groups of poems and essays which are known to be widely read by students. The emphasis is on clarification and evaluation; biographical and historical facts, while they may be discussed when they throw light on particular elements in a writer's work, are generally subordinated to critical discussion. What kind of work is this? What exactly goes on here? How good is this work, and why? These are the questions that each writer will try to answer.

It should be emphasized that these studies are written on the assumption that the reader has already read carefully the work discussed. The objective is not to enable students to deliver opinions about works they have not read, nor is it to provide ready-made ideas to be applied to works that have been read. In one sense all critical interpretation can be regarded as foisting opinions on readers, but to accept this is to deny the advantages of any sort of critical discussion directed at students or indeed at anybody else. The aim of these studies is to provide what Coleridge called in another context 'aids to reflection' about the works discussed. The interpretations are offered as suggestive rather than as definitive, in the hope of stimulating the reader into developing further his own insights. This is after all the function of all critical discourse among sensible people.

David Daiches

Contents

Introduction

So our virtues
Lie in th' interpretation of the time.   (IV.vii.49f)

Coriolanus is Shakespeare's most difficult, most complex play. It has often been misunderstood and has never been very popular. A. C. Bradley, writing in 1912, observed that it was 'seldom acted, and perhaps no reader ever called it his favourite play'. T. S. Eliot's riposte, in 1919, when he bracketed it with *Antony and Cleopatra* as 'Shakespeare's most assured artistic success', has been largely dismissed as a puzzling gesture of defiance which Eliot was never able to elaborate on. Recently T. J. B. Spencer has said that 'to write *Coriolanus* was one of the great feats of the historical imagination in Renaissance Europe', and although this is a just comment the play is far more than a historical feat. It is Shakespeare's most detailed analysis of politics, an analysis carried out both at the public level—the formal political manoeuvring between the patricians and the plebeians over the rulers' attempt to have Coriolanus elected consul; and, at the personal level, within the family, in the relationship between Coriolanus and his mother, Volumnia. In both spheres the analysis is presented by Shakespeare but is not explicitly judged by him. All the information is given to us, but the dramatist does not vote for one side or the other. He votes, I shall argue, against both sides, but this is an interpretation of the play that has not often been made. Critics have usually sided with the people, or with the rulers; but whatever their position on this issue they have mostly sided against Coriolanus.

One reason for the great divergence of opinion about this tragedy—greater than for any other of Shakespeare's mature plays—is its withholding of explicit judgement; another is the subtlety with which Shakespeare worked, a subtlety that has been lost on many of the commentators. While it will always be a difficult play, 'caviar to the general', and may never mean much to people who have not been accustomed to think critically about politics and about such issues as the manipulation of a democracy and the pressurization of the individual, one could at least have expected that trained scholars and critics would perceive the subtlety with which Shakespeare balanced his hero's virtues and faults. Yet the dominant reaction of his critics in this century (to go no further back) has been unfavourable. To A. C. Bradley, who conceded him some 'nobleness of nature', Coriolanus was none the less 'the proudest man in Shakespeare', 'an impossible person', whose 'faults are repellent and chill our sympathy'. He has been described as 'a schoolboy, crazed with notions of privilege and social distinction' (Wyndham Lewis), as 'essentially the splendid oaf who has never come to maturity' (J. Palmer), or as 'inordinately proud, and rather a schoolboy' (K. Muir). If not proud or adolescent he has been accused of being too much the soldier, dehumanizing himself in the pursuit of military success: one critic described him as a 'human war-machine', a 'mechanical warrior, a man turned into an instrument of war' (D. A. Traversi); another saw him as a 'mechanical juggernaut' (D. J. Enright), yet another as 'an automaton in flight, a slaying-machine of mechanic excellence' (G. W. Knight). Implicit in all these accounts is an unsympathetic attitude to the hero; one critic, indeed, suggested that Coriolanus was in fact alienated from us by Shakespeare, as a deliberate effect of tragic satire (O. J. Campbell).

Yet, fashionable though 'alienation' may be as an aesthetic concept, it does not seem relevant to Shakespearian tragedy in general, nor does it apply to this play. In none of the mature tragedies are we asked to remain wholly detached from the central tragic character, uninvolved with his goals, their frustration, and his suffering; nor are we expected to be detached from Coriolanus. If we entirely fail to sympathize with him, we have misunderstood the play. I shall argue that he is a character, and his is a situation, which are fully tragic because they exist in a context in which a profound conflict of values renders individual action, and finally existence itself, impossible and pointless.

In order to do justice to Shakespeare's subtlety we have to separate and define each of the areas of pressure on Coriolanus which he has fused so organically; we must see each area for what it represents in itself, before putting it back into the fluid movement of the play as a whole. Two great critical errors in reading *Coriolanus* have been to take a person or social group either at their own estimate of themselves or at others' estimate of them. Another error has been to take a character out of its social context, and to attribute to it alone ideas or attitudes which are in fact the responsibility of the class to which it belongs. Lump those three errors together, I suggest, and you have an explanation for the generally unsympathetic response to Coriolanus. His pride, arrogance, unfeelingness, machine-like military destructiveness, ingratitude, and so forth, the qualities harped on by many modern critics, are all misconceptions loosely derived from what people *say* about Coriolanus, not what he *does*.

This play makes a deep analysis of action and value; so do all Shakespeare's tragedies, and indeed all major works of literature. What is exceptional about *Coriolanus* is that it also analyses the evaluation of action and value, the processes by which human behaviour is seen by others, reported on by them, given an agreed status or meaning. In other plays Shakespeare has used dramatic situations in which action was made to seem other than it was: in *Much Ado About Nothing* Claudio is made to see his wife-to-be, Hero, as a false, corrupt deceiver of him, and in *Othello* Iago imposes on Othello a vision and an evaluation of Desdemona that is a creation of fantasy and malice. In other plays, too, Shakespeare had presented critical moments of evaluation, from Portia's choice of the caskets to the discussions in *Troilus and Cressida* of value as a subjective, individual reaction and as an objective, social one. To Troilus' question 'What's aught but as 'tis valued?' Hector replies:

> But value dwells not in particular will;
> It holds his estimate and dignity
> As well wherein 'tis precious of itself
> As in the prizer. (II.ii.53ff)

Coriolanus pushes that debate further, deeper into the issue, both at the individual and the social levels. How does a man learn values? What do they mean to him? What happens if you ask him to change them? Those are some of the questions that will face Coriolanus. For his society the questions are more disturbing: how can you best create a value? To what extent can an image of value be manipulated? If each political group has its own interpretation of events, which one is right? Whom can we trust?

In approaching *Coriolanus*, then, I urge that we consider its evaluations of human action as we would do in real life. To evaluate human behaviour we tend to use a scale running from 'good' to 'bad', but we know that different people will give different evaluations of the same act. We know that values are personal, and that other people may have entirely different categories to ours. When person A tells us something nice, or nasty, about person B, we do not mechanically accept it as an objective fact: we know that it has been coloured by the personality and values of person A, and we will accept or reject it according to our evaluation of them. We all know, furthermore, that people do not communicate with us in total openness, honesty and candour, addressing themselves purely to the matter in hand in itself and for itself. They often speak or act in the present with an eye to some future state or event; they wish us to see or think or do something according to their wills or plans, not ours. They have, as we say, a 'design' on us. If we subsequently realize that the design was a harmless one which resulted in mutual pleasure and profit with no evil effects, then we are not likely to mind. But if we realize that we have been made to do something that we did not wish to do, and especially if we have been made to do something degrading or humiliating to ourselves and others, then we will feel cheated, exploited, manipulated.

I have written that very simple account of evaluation, presentation and manipulation in real life partly because I feel that modern criticism is in danger of severing its links with ordinary human behaviour, and partly because *Coriolanus* presents just these patterns of action as they affect a hero who lives in a state of pristine innocence. This will be Coriolanus' first experience of a conflict of values or an opposition between loyalties; his first experience of manipulation; and, above all, his first experience of politics. What makes the play so complicated and so hard to evaluate, is that on to my simple model of human behaviour Shakespeare has superimposed the whole system of political evaluation, political presentation and political manipulation. This not only complicates the issue but makes it more uncertain, unstable. For in addition to the inevitable clash between individual value-judgements, we have the clash between those of political parties, with their 'agreed values', values which can nevertheless be changed or abandoned if politically expedient; 'agreed fictions', we might call them, images which are created precisely in order to manipulate. Political parties are supposed to address themselves to immediate issues; they are supposed to work for the good of the whole community. This play shows the opposite practices, action addressed to some concealed aim, and action designed to secure and advance the power of a party in itself and for itself, if necessary against the community.

Politics is one of the areas of existence in which Coriolanus is made to act, and his actions observed, evaluated and reported on, sometimes to one end, sometimes to another. There are three other areas in which the same process of action, report and evaluation are carried out: Coriolanus in war and fighting; Coriolanus in relation to his class; Coriolanus in relation to his family. In all four Coriolanus is the focus of action and commentary. If we use the familar division between 'individual' and 'society' we would have to say that the individual here is not merely juxtaposed with society but that the pressures of this society—above all the conflicting demands of class, politics and family—are not only seen acting on Coriolanus but *can only express themselves in and through him*. They conflict with each other not face to face but through him. The central experience of the play is of a man caught in the various social roles that we all hold, simultaneously, each with its own loyalties—as son, husband, father, to the family; as soldier, to his comrades and his social rank; as political man to the party of his class—a man caught in these roles and destroyed by the conflict between them. At the end of the play all the social groups—aristocrats, plebeians, the family, the arm , the enemy—are recognizably the same as they were at the beginning: only Coriolanus is dead.

Coriolanus is the centre of the play, the focal point towards which every pressure converges. For this reason his character is under constant discussion from all groups, and a mass of conflicting evaluations of him can soon be assembled. Yet it is not enough to say that Shakespeare intends there to be a final 'mystery' about him. Each evaluation tells us as much, if not more, about the person or group making it than about Coriolanus himself. There are no unbiased opinions about him, each is the product of an implicit social attitude or an explicit social goal. Finally the only evaluation of him that matters is his own: what he values, how he acts and how he evaluates his own action, are, in the last resort, the most important human judgements. As Kierkegaard said, 'a man lives his values.' But even here we cannot accept his perspective alone, for neither his actions nor his evaluations of them are purely personal discoveries. At the crisis of the play, when he is vainly trying to deny his instinctual love and loyalty to his family, he cries out

> I'll never
> Be such a gosling to obey instinct, but stand
> As if a man were author of himself
> And knew no other kin. (V.iii.34ff)

But the linguistic formulation itself ('As if . . . were') denies its own validity. Coriolanus, like any other man, is in part a product of his society and his family, with all their ideals and prejudices, inhibitions and taboos, evasions and self-flattery. Critics who isolate Coriolanus from his social nexus fail to see how much of his character has been learned, acquired. Yet, before we start to examine that social nexus, let us guard against fall-

ing into the opposite error, of making him entirely homogeneous with
the values of his class and family. Coriolanus has learned much from
them, but the more he sees what they have made of him the more he
tries to unlearn it. One of the least commented on aspects of the play, and
the one that, in my view, gives Coriolanus an independent and tragic
existence, is the process by which he frees himself to the point where he
is no longer of any use either to his class or to his family, so that they can
afford to sacrifice him in order to preserve themselves.

1 *Class War*

The Rome of *Coriolanus* is a society at war, both externally, against the
Volscians, and internally, against itself. Given this existence, the values of
the ruling class are exclusively aggressive, self-defending and self-
perpetuating. In reading Plutarch Shakespeare found an explanation of
Roman society at that period which he has built into the play not only as
an almost verbatim quotation but as a characterization of a whole class
strikingly lacking in any other qualities but those designed to give
immediate and continuing success in combat, military or civil:

> Now in those dayes, valliantnesse was honoured in Rome above all
> other vertues: which they called *Virtus*, by the name of vertue selfe,
> as including in that generall name, all other speciall vertues besides.
> (ed. G. Bullough, 506)[1]

In the play these sentiments are given to Cominius, at the start of his
formal panegyric on Coriolanus' achievements at Corioli:

> It is held
> That valour is the chiefest virtue *and*
> *Most dignifies the haver*   (II.ii.81ff; my italics)

What Shakespeare has added is the attitude often expressed by the
patricians in this play, their awareness of appearances, of the beneficial
results of heroism, how a man's image—and so his political bargaining

[1] Full details of all references, where not given in the text, can be found in the
Bibliography.

power—will be enhanced by fame or glory, how these will 'become' him. That is, the patricians tend to evaluate action not so much in itself but for its future benefits to them. They always have an eye to what they can get out of it.

Coriolanus has certainly taken over from his class a belief in the value of the soldier and of such military virtues as courage, loyalty, and comradeship. But for Coriolanus valour is not the chief, nor the only virtue, and even valour is pursued by him in an idealistic, non-materialistic way. He fights not because fighting is an end in itself, nor for his own profit, but out of love for his country, service to the state. This is made clear to us in the sequence of scenes presenting the battle for Corioli, and its aftermath (especially I.vi and I.ix).

Highlighting this part of the play reveals a fairly simple, unproblematic relationship. Coriolanus could go on fighting for the good of Rome for just as long as he could stand up. Yet this Rome is not a united and self-balancing society, but one divided by famine and social unrest. Shakespeare chooses to begin the play with a mob, up in arms and angry for food, convinced that the patricians are withholding grain from them. The patricians send Menenius to them in his role as friend of the people, as they have done before, and he manages to placate them once again with the old story about the belly, a part of the body which *appears* to do no work—like the senators of Rome, he argues—but in fact supports the rest of the organism or state (I.i.88ff). It is, as Menenius says, a tale that 'serves my purpose', but this is the last time that he will be able to fob the people off, for under the pressure of their protests, we learn, the patricians have just granted the people five tribunes to represent their case (I.i.214ff). When told of this by Coriolanus, Menenius comments, 'This is strange': evidently so liberal a gesture puzzles the more reactionary party.

We are here at the beginning, in Rome, of an experiment in democracy and political representation. It goes hideously wrong, and although we must place the blame for this on the self-seeking nature of the tribunes and the stupidity of the people, a large element in the social discord—and just the one that the tribunes can exploit for their ends—is the patricians' general loathing of the people. Coriolanus' first words in the play constitute the most unattractive opening lines of any Shakespeare character:

> What's the matter, you dissentious rogues
> That, rubbing the poor itch of your opinion,
> Make yourselves scabs? (I.i.163ff)

It is undeniable that Coriolanus loathes the populace. But before we dismiss him as 'proud' or 'arrogant' we should consider two other factors that Shakespeare has rather carefully worked up throughout the play, sometimes in contradiction to his sources: first, the general patrician attitude to the plebs, and secondly, the plebs' actual behaviour in battle.

The leading patricians are Cominius, Menenius, and Volumnia: they are a coherent group ('us o'th' right-hand file' is how Menenius describes them (II.i.22), 'Enter Coriolanus . . . [and] all the Gentry' is how Shakespeare puts it in the stage direction to Act III, scene i), and they express a coherent attitude, one of disgust and contempt for the plebeians. Menenius calls them 'my countrymen' and 'friends' to their faces, avows that the patricians 'care for you like fathers' (I.i.54, 64, 76f), yet when the quarrelsome first citizen challenges him his real feelings break out:

> Rome and her rats are at the point of battle;
> The one side must have bale.   (I.i.161f)

There is no doubt which side will 'have bale', or be destroyed. The metaphor of 'rats' to describe the people is used to introduce the desired reflex: 'exterminate them'. Menenius dismisses the tribunes with a similarly insulting reduction of the people to the level of animals: they are 'the herdsmen of the beastly plebeians' (II.i.93f). By this point in the play we have few illusions about the goodness of the citizens, yet all the same Menenius' contempt is nauseating, as when he describes the people as 'multiplying spawn' (II.ii.76). Here person A's evaluation of group B can only reduce our sympathy for person A. Yet members of this patrician class support one another in these attitudes: when Coriolanus rages at the people Menenius calls it a 'worthy rage' (III.i.240); a nobleman approves of Coriolanus' refusal to compromise: 'You do the nobler' (III.ii.6); Volumnia says that Coriolanus is 'too absolute', although therein he 'can never be too noble' (III.ii.39f). Even the more restrained Cominius describes the people as a 'tag', or rabble (III.i.247), and Menenius sees this class as 'the grains', the tribunes as 'the musty chaff' (V.i.30f).

The most revealing expression of the patricians' hatred for the people comes out when Coriolanus puzzles over Volumnia's eagerness that he should flatter the people in order to gain their votes for the consulship:

> I muse my mother
> Does not approve me further, who was wont
> To call them woollen vassals, things created
> To buy and sell with groats; to show bare heads

> In congregations, to yawn, be still and wonder,
> When one but of my ordinance stood up
> To speak of peace or war. (III.ii.7ff)

This sequence creates an effect which we experience several times in this play, that of a sudden insight into past or future behaviour: people are recorded, unawares, in some peculiarly revealing posture. There we have the whole ethos of aristocratic superiority that Coriolanus has been born into and moulded by. Volumnia in the present is just as violent, for when her son says of the people, 'Let them hang', she adds 'Ay, and burn too' (III.ii.23f). At Coriolanus' banishment she calls down the typhus on them:

> Now the red pestilence strike all trades in Rome,
> And occupations perish! (IV.i.14f)

Added to the violence of the wish is the unpleasant aristocrat's definition of its enemies as being all those who have to work for a living ('occupations'). Surely we cannot endorse the patricians on this issue.

As for Coriolanus' attitude to the people, it is the same as the rest of his class, only expressed with the energy and vehemence that he brings to all his activities. It bulks larger, then, both in quantity and intensity, than that of the other patricians. The people, he says, 'would feed on one another' if their rulers did not keep them under control (I.i.186f). 'Hang 'em!' is his remedy (I.i.180, 203). He describes them as 'fragments' (I.i.221), 'Our musty superfluity' (224), 'rats' (248); he loathes their dirty faces and stinking breath (II.iii.59f), they are the 'rank-scented meiny' (III.i.66), 'measles' or scabs 'Which we disdain should tetter us' (78f); they are 'The beast / With many heads' (IV.i.1f). The culmination of all his feelings towards them is his speech after they have banished him:

> You common cry of curs! whose breath I hate
> As reek o'th' rotten fens, whose loves I prize
> As the dead carcasses of unburied men
> That do corrupt my air—I banish you. (III.iii.120ff)

It is hard to think of many more unpleasant similes than that.

It would be a failure of humanity if the reader, spectator, or critic did not register at this point an unequivocal distaste for the patricians' violent feelings against the citizens who, after all, represent the bulk of their country and on whose work and services they rely in order to support their own positions of privilege. If Shakespeare now were to show the people as not having the faults ascribed to them, but as being honest, sober, responsible craftsmen, workers of integrity—then we could safely dismiss the patricians as the villains of the piece. But he does no such thing. He presents them as muddled and confused, as in the scene where a group of them on stage together, with neither patricians to abuse nor tribunes to organize them, are made to undermine their own pretensions to having a coherent collective identity:

> *1 Citizen.* . . . [Coriolanus] stuck not to call us the many-headed multitude.
> *3 Citizen.* We have been called so of many; not that our heads are some brown, some black, some abram, some bald, but that our wits are so diversely coloured: and truly I think, if all our wits were to issue out of one skull, they would fly east, west, north, south, and their consent of one direct way should be at once to all the points o'th' compass. (II.iii.15ff)[*]

Evidently Shakespeare does not intend us to think very highly of the mob. (Where Plutarch records that their protest against the famine took the form of a peaceful and religious gesture, leaving the town to go as suppliants to a sacred hill, Shakespeare will allow them no contact with the sacred, and makes them mutinous, not peaceful.) Even the tribunes, their own leaders, despise them—whenever, that is, they do not do exactly what the tribunes expect of them. So Brutus describes the people's welcome to Coriolanus with such contempt that one might be forgiven for recalling the lines as having been spoken by one of the patricians. The mob is so eager to see him, he reports, that the 'prattling nurse' neglects her child to gossip about him:

> the kitchen malkin pins
> Her richest lockram 'bout her reechy neck,
> Clamb'ring the walls to eye him: stalls, bulks, windows,
> Are smothered up, leads filled and ridges horsed
> With variable complexions, all agreeing
> In earnestness to see him.   (II.i.202ff)

The images of dirt and commotion, the sardonic oxymoron of 'richest lockram', the contemptuous punning sound (richest/reechy), the deliberately ugly and undignified verbs to describe the crowd's movement (clamb'ring, smothered up, horsed)—the language reduces their own supporters to an animal-like jumble. From this and other comments by the tribunes it is impossible to take the people seriously as an alternative to the patricians: we cannot prefer either.

The really telling factor in the disvaluing of the people, and one that relates most closely to Coriolanus' own set of values, involves a substantial change made by Shakespeare of his sources. In Plutarch's account the people of Rome are not, perhaps, such dedicated soldiers as Coriolanus but they fight alongside him, rallying to his calls. Although there are 'very fewe men to helpe him' in Corioli they do fight on with him, and his subsequent exhortation moves the whole army to fight once more (Bullough, 511–14). His only criticism of them is directed against the looters. In Shakespeare the people are much less reliable. Even before the battle of Corioli, Martius sums up their previous behaviour in terms which make it clear to us that they stand as polar opposites to all his values: they are 'curs', who are frightened by war but in peacetime become 'proud' (that is, referring to animals, 'quarrelsome, high-mettled, ungovernable').

> He that trusts to you,
> Where he should find you lions, finds you hares; . . .
> He that depends
> Upon your favours swims with fins of lead
> And hews down oaks with rushes. Hang ye! Trust ye?
> With every minute you do change a mind,
> And call him noble that was now your hate,
> Him vile that was your garland.   (I.i.167ff, 178ff)

Although it is excessively violent, as usual, the inescapable fact about that speech is that Shakespeare has so planned the play that every criticism in it is justified. The mob are cowardly; they go to war not out of Coriolanus' ideals of service to their country but only when they cannot avoid the duty. When Coriolanus and the other patricians are about to leave for the wars Shakespeare makes the populace slink off: '*citizens steal away*' is his stage direction, and Coriolanus comments with sarcasm:

> Worshipful mutineers,
> Your valour puts well forth.   (I.i.249f)

That is, it 'makes a fine show'. Finally at the wars, if the plebeians can make any profit by looting, they will; and in peacetime they are fickle and unreliable.

They are so constructed by Shakespeare as to form an anti-type to Coriolanus' values—or he is so built up as to be their opposite. When the

Roman soldiers are beaten back ignominiously—a detail invented by Shakespeare—he attacks them as 'geese':

> how have you run
> From slaves that apes would beat! Pluto and hell!
> All hurt behind! backs red and faces pale
> With flight and agued fear!   (I.iv.34ff)

He tries to rally them with his favourite idea of 'standing': 'If you'll stand fast, we'll beat them to their wives' (41). But they take 'stand' literally, remaining where they are outside Corioli while Martius breaks into the city alone. 'Mark me, and do the like', he cries, and they reply:

> *1 Soldier.* Fool-hardiness; not I.
> *2 Soldier.* Nor I.   [*Martius is shut in*
> *1 Soldier.* See, they have shut him in.
> *All.*   To th'pot, I warrant him.   (I.iv.46ff)

The callousness of that final image—leaving him to be chopped up in the stew-pot—is observed by us, and not by Coriolanus, so that when the mob of soldiers descend to looting instead of fighting we can hardly not endorse his attack on their greed for trash:

> See here these movers that do prize their honours
> At a cracked drachma! Cushions, leaden spoons,
> Irons of a doit, doublets that hangmen would
> Bury with those that wore them, these base slaves,
> Ere yet the fight be done, pack up.   (I.v.4ff)

Nor can we quarrel with his later description of the people's cowardice: 'The mouse ne'er shunned the cat as they did budge / From rascals worse than they' (I.vi.43f). Commentators have praised Shakespeare for his refusal to take sides, and Coleridge enthused over the 'wonderful impartiality in Shakespeare's politics'. What needs to be said, however, is that Shakespeare has downgraded both sides, successively eliminating each party as an object of our sympathy or concern.

2 Political Image-making

Moving now from the opposed social groups to the individual who is the focus of their conflict, we begin to notice that when set against his family or class Coriolanus exists not as a free individual but as a man with a role to play on behalf of others. His mother claims credit for the self-sacrifice by which she sent him, when still a boy, to 'a cruel war' in order to 'find fame' (I.iii.13), and she refers possessively to him as 'my boy Martius . . . my good soldier. . . . My gentle Martius' (II.i.98, 169f). After Coriolanus has gone to see the patricians on his return from Corioli, Volumnia reveals her longstanding ambition that her son should become consul:

> I have lived
> To see inherited my very wishes
> And the buildings of my fancy: only
> There's one thing wanting, which I doubt not but
> Our Rome will cast upon thee.   (II.i.195ff)

She has 'long dreamed of an inheritance', as the editors gloss the second line: the fantasy which she has indulged in is about to come true. Yet she speaks as if the inheritance will be hers, not his; and the disproportion in the pronouns (four 'I' or 'my' to one 'our' and one 'thee') reflects the sense we receive that Coriolanus has been groomed for success for her sake, not his own. He will fulfil the desires which she, as a woman, could not fulfil (see D. W. Harding's article). As he says, with some resentment, at the moment of banishment: 'Mother, you wot well / My hazards still have been your solace' (IV.i.27f). Whatever he imagines he is doing, he is in effect a puppet, being controlled by her.

Within the patrician class he is also a puppet. In this rather confused political situation, where power has been given to the people and its representatives, yet with no clear division of responsibility for the legislature and the executive, the sole strategy of the patricians is to have Coriolanus elected consul, from which position, they imagine, he will be able to exert their traditional downward pressure over the people. The main justification for his election being his military feats on behalf of the state, we see the patricians again and again building up an image of Coriolanus as an invincible fighter. Modern critics have noted the presence of these passages but have mostly failed to see their significance as political propaganda in an election-campaign. As a result such critics describe Coriolanus as a juggernaut or tank, as if that were the evaluation Shakespeare were making of him. In fact, however, Shakespeare evidently evaluates him favourably as a soldier who fights for his country to the limits of endurance, and just as clearly indicates the gap between a balanced evaluation of Coriolanus and the extraordinary reports that the patricians give of him. In the mouths of the patricians any chance to report on Coriolanus' deeds becomes the occasion for shameless panegyrics, encomia produced with an eye to his vote-catching power as superhero.

When Martius is shut up alone inside Corioli, and seems lost, Lartius pronounces a premature epitaph over him which shows the instinctive patrician desire to exaggerate his exploits:

> Thou wast a soldier
> Even to Cato's wish, not fierce and terrible
> Only in strokes; but with thy grim looks and
> The thunder-like percussion of thy sounds
> Thou mad'st thine enemies shake, as if the world
> Were feverous and did tremble.   (I.iv.57ff)

The magnification of Coriolanus by the patricians results always in a kind of gigantism: his voice is now like thunder, enemies quake before him as if he gave the whole world the jitters. All these 'enormous and disgusting hyperboles' (as Dr Johnson described the Metaphysicals' conceits) are quite disproportionate to what we see of Coriolanus, or indeed of any man. The political function of it all is nakedly revealed just after the battle, where Cominius looks forward to 'reporting' his exploits precisely for the social and political effect they will have. Each section of society (he hopes) will react with admiration and gratitude:

> If I should tell thee o'er this thy day's work,
> Thou't not believe thy deeds: but I'll report it
> Where senators shall mingle tears with smiles;
> Where great patricians shall attend, and shrug,
> I'th' end admire; where ladies shall be frighted,
> And, gladly quaked, hear more; where the dull tribunes,

> That with the fusty plebeians hate thine honours,
> Shall say against their hearts 'We thank the gods
> Our Rome hath such a soldier'.   (I.ix.1ff)

Before we see the triumph-scene, and before we know whether or not Cominius' report will have the effect he hopes for, Shakespeare brings together Menenius and Volumnia, who have received news of Coriolanus' success in the battle. As they discuss his fortunes the patrician concept of his 'person' or body as an investment-object is rendered literal, quantified before our eyes; wounds, like honour, 'become' him, not just in themselves but for their vote-catching power.

> *Menenius.* Is he not wounded? he was wont to come home wounded.
> *Virgilia.* O, no, no, no.
> *Volumnia.* O, he is wounded; I thank the gods for't.
> *Menenius.* So do I too, if it be not too much. Brings a' victory in his pocket, the wounds become him. . . . Where is he wounded?
> *Volumnia.* I'th'shoulder and i'th'left arm: there will be large cicatrices to show the people, when he shall stand for his place.
>
> (II.i.116ff, 144ff)

Volumnia truly has Coriolanus' body, and his career, mapped out for him, and to her the fact that he now has 27 visible scars proves his invincibility in war and peace. As I have written elsewhere, 'they count his scars, each one fatal to the enemy, with the same intention as that of the soldier or confirmed killer making notches on the handle of a gun or a knife. Coriolanus is their human liquidator.' (Vickers, pp. 395f)

In the triumph-scene itself we can observe the formation of a marketable political image, for Cominius' panegyric to Coriolanus takes on a unity and identity in itself which has less and less connection with the man we have observed. Menenius formally invites Cominius 'to report/A little of that worthy work performed' by Coriolanus (II.ii.42ff), but his 'little' is swept aside by a Senator, who urges Cominius to 'Leave nothing out for length' (47ff). The purpose of this zealous invitation is again made explicit by Shakespeare as the senator addresses the tribunes:

> We do request your kindest ears; and, after,
> Your loving motion toward the common body,
> To yield what passes here.   (50ff)

The patricians are naïve enough to think that the tribunes will pass on their panegyrics as reported: that is one of the weak links in their strategy.

Thus prompted, Cominius launches into a forty-line speech reviewing Coriolanus' glowing career down to the present. If we pick out the account of the battle of Corioli we will see the disproportion between the event and the analogies used to describe it, in which a man is elevated to the level of some principle of death by being depersonalized, successively treated as a ship, a tool for stamping a mark on some softer material, a blood-covered machine:

> as weeds before
> A vessel under sail, so men obeyed,
> And fell below his stem. His sword, death's stamp,
> Where it did mark, it took; from face to foot
> He was a thing of blood, whose every motion
> Was timed with dying cries.   (I.ix.28f)

The unity of attitude and intention among the patricians is shown again by the similarity between this and the scene just before, where Volumnia and Menenius created their image of Coriolanus as death-machine.

> *Menenius*. Now it's twenty-seven [wounds]: every gash was an enemy's grave.—Hark! the trumpets.
> *Volumnia*. These are the ushers of Martius. Before him he carries noise, and behind him he leaves tears:
> Death, that dark spirit, in's nervy arm doth lie.
> Which, being advanced, declines, and then men die.
> (II.i.153ff)

The antithesis and paradox in the last line creates the same impression as Cominius' 'every motion . . . timed with dying cries', the impression of a stiff, unstoppable machine, with a jerky action, 'up: down: dead!', each movement a killing one. But this is to coin an image of Coriolanus as some supernatural force with whom death is in league, while we know that Coriolanus is only a man. In other words the visions tell us more about the patricians and their need to create a gigantic, frightening image of Coriolanus to represent their own power, their own wished-for deterrent. Cominius even describes him as running 'reeking o'er the lives of men, as if / 'Twere a perpetual spoil' (II.ii.116ff), that is, at once a stream of blood swallowing up the men in his path and a predatory animal massacring deer. The image of Coriolanus created by the patricians is nauseating, disclosing their pathological delight in blood and death, and their desire to have a superman figure on their side.

In this way the two areas of society closest to Coriolanus, the family and the patricians, see him as performing the major role in their own triumphs, and in order to give this role a prestige matching their ambitions they do not hesitate to inflate 'report' until it overtowers reality. How does Coriolanus react? If he were the proud and arrogant figure described by some modern critics he would presumably revel in all this, gloat over his defeated enemies, bask in adulation. In fact he does quite the opposite. I have made the general claim that Coriolanus, on some major issues, stands outside the values of his class, and this is one of them. He does not at all share the ambition that Volumnia has for him. After her speech looking forward to the fulfilment of her greatest desire he affirms that his values are more important to him than the power, and values, of others:

> Know, good mother,
> I had rather be their servant in my way
> Than sway with them in theirs. (II.i.199ff)

As a reply to a mother in her ecstasy of longing that is cool enough: indeed, if we watch Coriolanus each time he refers to his mother we will find him not lacking in duty, of course, but often expressing a certain resentment at her demands on him and on his behalf. One of the most carefully developed pieces of characterization that Shakespeare ever made is Coriolanus' loathing of adulation. At his first appearance Menenius welcomes him fervently: 'Hail, noble Martius!', and gets as reply the laconic 'Thanks' (I.i.162f). When Lartius expresses concern at his wounds the reply is simply, 'Sir, praise me not' (I.v.16). Later, the battle successful, Lartius embarks on a panegyric, with Coriolanus as 'the steed, we the caparison' only to be cut short with:

> Pray now, no more: my mother,
> Who has a charter to extol her blood,
> When she does praise me grieves me. (I.ix.13ff)

The sarcasm in that remark ('my mother has taken out a licence to praise her own family') is repeated when he is welcomed by her at the triumph:

> *All.* Welcome to Rome, renownéd Coriolanus!
> *Coriolanus.* No more of this, it does offend my heart;
> Pray now, no more.
> *Cominius.* Look, sir, your mother!
> *Coriolanus.*   O, [*kneels*

You have, I know, petitioned all the gods
For my prosperity!   (II.i.165ff)

'That's what you've been up to again': the note of disapproval of her
vociferousness on behalf of her own family is unmistakable. Coriolanus
shares the sense of social superiority common to his whole class, but he
does not share their pride, ambition, or liking for adulation. It is hard to
see how critics can have failed to note the quantity and intensity of anti-
panegyrical feelings given to Coriolanus. At every point where his deeds
are vaunted he responds with violent disapproval. His characteristic
reaction to praise is embarrassment—he blushes; at the same time he tries
to minimize his exploits and deflate the praise-situation. In the scene after
Corioli, Cominius urges him not to be 'the grave' of his 'deserving';
Coriolanus' reply is a brief disclaimer:

> I have some wounds upon me, and they smart
> To hear themselves rememb'red.   (I.ix.28f)

But for once Shakespeare is not ready to let it go at that. Since this
sequence < action : evaluation : report : adulation : advantage > is
crucial to the political manoeuvering in the play he devotes 80 lines of this
scene to a debate on the morality of praise and reward. Cominius offers
Coriolanus a tenth of the spoils as a reward for his bravery, and when the
offer is refused as unnecessary the soldiers give their hero a great
acclamation. The army's reactions to Coriolanus' integrity may seem
perfectly reasonable to us: if so, we will be quite unprepared for the
violence, the almost religious feeling of sacrilege with which Coriolanus
attacks his comrades:

> May these same instruments which you profane
> Never sound more! When drums and trumpets shall
> I'th'field prove flatterers, let courts and cities be
> Made all of false-faced soothing!   (41ff)

This shows a truly deep loathing, a suspicion of panegyric as expressing
flattery and lies, an inherently false genre:

> You shout me forth
> In acclamations hyperbolical;
> As if I loved my little should be dieted
> In praises sauced with lies.   (50ff)

They do 'cry him up', and their hyperboles do topple over into fiction and fantasy.

With great insistence Shakespeare builds up this picture of a soldier embarrassed and nauseated by praise, who tends in response to undervalue his own exploits. Coriolanus does not seem to be aware why his class praises him so much, but he finds their praise out of proportion to his deeds. He is not, then, a 'proud' man, in terms of his personal achievements. Indeed when Cominius delivers his formal panegyric Coriolanus cannot bear to listen to it:

> I had rather have one scratch my head i'th'sun
> When the alarum were struck than idly sit
> To hear my nothings monstered.   (II.ii.73ff)

If not proud, neither is he ambitious. Having engaged to serve with Cominius he is ready to honour his promise, and accepts his place below him (I.i.236ff). As we have seen, he would rather be a servant of Rome on his terms than have power on theirs (II.i.199ff). He does not in the least wish to be consul, and tries several times to get released from the task—but the patricians insist.

All this is perfectly clear. Yet in the play he is called proud and ambitious, and some modern critics have taken over those criticisms without realizing that Shakespeare has disvalued them by giving them to the enemies of Coriolanus. Those people who resent him wish to abuse him and therefore call him proud. The tribunes even accuse him of ambition, but Shakespeare makes them do so immediately after we have seen him gladly accept the post subordinate to Cominius:

> *Brutus.* The present wars devour him! He is grown
> Too proud to be so valiant.
>   *Sicinius.*   Such a nature,
> Tickled with good success, disdains the shadow
> Which he treads on at noon. But I do wonder
> His insolence can brook to be commanded
> Under Cominius.
>   *Brutus.*   Fame, at the which he aims

and so on, speculating how Martius will rob Cominius of his merits (I.i.257ff). The tribunes are inventing this greed for fame and precedence, which does not square with anything we have seen of Coriolanus. What in effect is happening is that they, too, are constructing an agreed image of Coriolanus for their own purposes. In order to succeed with the people they have to create a figure that will absorb all the class-hatred and resentment of the plebeians. Of course, given Martius' personally violent endorsement of the patricians' sense of superiority, that is not a difficult task. Yet their manner of executing it involves constant distortions. After we have seen the vehemence with which Coriolanus has rejected the army's tributes to him at Corioli and the nausea he revealed at their boasting about him, the tribunes' account of him is exposed as the product of cheap malice:

> *Brutus.* He's poor in no one fault, but stored with all.
> *Sicinius.* Especially in pride.
> *Brutus.* And topping all others in boasting.   (II.i.18ff)

Their Coriolanus is a caricature of all 'anti-democratic attitudes'. It is the creation, as are all the other images of Coriolanus in the play, of immediate needs and long-term political ambition. Their underlying political motives emerge in their dialogue at the end of the scene where he returns in triumph to Rome:

> *Sicinius.*   On the sudden,
> I warrant him consul.
> *Brutus.*   Then our office may
> During his power go sleep.   (II.i.218ff)

To preserve their power they will try to destroy his—that being one of the operative principles in politics, then as now. Their 'identikit' picture of Coriolanus is almost a parody of the clichés about the upper classes so necessary to the continuance of class hatred.It is one of the sharper, and sadder, insights of this play that social divisions based on class enmity need to create ever more violent images of the enemy if the class struggle is to continue. These are tragic divisions.

3 Rehearsals and Performance

In any political situation where conflicting interpretations of events oppose each other in the struggle for immediate power, the resulting actions can be described as a sequence of consolidation, manipulation and direct attack. Each group has to unify its endeavours; each has to persuade its supporters that the cause is just; each has to rehearse its candidates in the appropriate role; and each has to exert prolonged and increasing pressure on the candidate and supporters of the other side. The central sequence in Acts II and III of *Coriolanus* resembles a gigantic two-party election, fought according to the usual political rules of magnification of one's own party and denigration of the other. Coriolanus is the protagonist on one side, organized and rehearsed by the patricians, while on the other the tribunes groom their protagonist, the mob. (As well as resembling an election campaign this sequence recalls two rival theatre-productions.)

As we have seen from their estimation of the bargaining-power of Coriolanus' wounds, the patricians are not lacking in calculation. But, more important, neither are the tribunes, and throughout Acts II and III Brutus and Sicinius dominate the action, manipulating it all from behind the scenes. That is, 'behind the scenes' as far as the patricians are concerned, but 'before them' as far as we are, for in this play Shakespeare makes a brilliantly sustained exploitation of drama's ability to mount separate presentation. Individual units of action presented onstage are experienced by some characters but not by others. We, the privileged spectators, see every stage in every group's preparations, but Coriolanus sees none of them. Once he has left the battlefield, where action is immediate and significant on its own terms, he enters a political arena in which every action that reaches him has been planned, rehearsed, set up entirely in terms of the effect it will have on his role or behaviour. He does not see his mother exulting over his bloody deeds (I.iii.), nor Volumnia and Menenius computing his wounds (II.i.); he does not hear the comments and evaluations made of him by the citizens (I.i.), by the two officers laying cushions in the Capitol (II.ii.), by the patricians in his temporary absence (III.i.), by Aufidius (I.x.; IV.vii.). So much of the action of the play *goes on behind Coriolanus' back*—we may say, dropping the conventions of literary criticism for a moment, and restoring the point-of-view of life—that it is no wonder if he seems completely puzzled by it all, unprepared to cope with what people say and do to him. In addition, each issue is no simple one, but always a crisis.

For much of the time (much more than for perhaps any character in any other play) Coriolanus is the focus of discussion and calculation. If two people meet in this play they will talk about him. In Act II, scene i, as a sinister epilogue to his triumph-scene, the two tribunes discuss for over 60 lines the tactics with which they will attack him when he stands for consul. They realize that he will loathe having to display his wounds (a practice of Elizabethan cast-off soldiers and beggars, often showing self-inflicted wounds—compare Edgar as 'Poor Tom' in *King Lear*, II.iii.14ff and Falstaff's tricks in *1 Henry IV*, II.iv.299ff), and then beg the people to give him their votes. They predict that if Coriolanus is once made angry he will be unable to control himself, a situation which they will be able to exploit, while they can be sure that the people, recalling their 'ancient malice' to Coriolanus, 'will forget/ With the least cause these his new honours' (224ff). The tribunes go off to the Capitol and use their power to force Coriolanus to go through with the ceremony (II.ii.133ff): as soon as he has left they again plot, behind his back, to work the people up against him (153ff).

The election ceremony takes place in the Forum (II.iii.): I call it a ceremony because it seems more like a rite than a truly open political choice. Coriolanus is the only candidate, supposedly representing the whole of Rome, but, in effect, standing for only part of it. In the intentions of the patricians the people are to be fobbed off with an upper-class candidate who will strengthen their own side and repress the people. They regard it as a mere formality for the people to endorse their candidate, and so ensure their future power, but Coriolanus sees it in the present, for what it does to his values, and he goes through with it in a mood of bitter jesting. He is standing for the office, he tells them, for his 'desert' but not his 'desire': ''twas never my desire yet to trouble the poor with begging' (61ff). In a soliloquy—for once he speaks behind somebody else's back—Coriolanus exposes the absurdity of the ceremony, for if he has already 'deserved' or earned the reward, why should he now have to 'crave' it? To do so suggests that the honours were not truly his in the first place, which is an insult, and it also suggests that the mob is a more valuable arbiter of honour than the standards of bravery and loyalty on the battlefield. The ceremony is a meaningless piece of ritual which serves only to confuse the true relationship between service and reward.

The people are expected to endorse the patricians' candidate, and although they presumably have a right to give a veto the ruling party never expects that they will exercise it. In the sequence between the tribunes and people that follows (II.iii.150–262) Shakespeare suddenly shows us how the tribunes carry out the political sequence which I have called consolidation, manipulation, and direct attack. It appears that the ceremony ought to have gone off quite differently, for the people had already been manipulated and rehearsed as to how they should have attacked. Whereas normally in this play we, the privileged spectators, see people and actions that Coriolanus does not see, here even we have not been allowed to attend this political rehearsal:

> *Brutus.* Could you not have told him—
> As you were lessoned— . . . .
>   You should have said. . . .
> *Sicinius.* Thus to have said,
> As you were fore-advised, had touched his spirit
> And tried his inclination. . . .   (II.iii.175f, 184, 189ff)

As they noted before leaving for the Capitol, provoking Coriolanus to anger is 'as easy/As to set dogs on sheep', and now they spell out the 'advantage' offered by the manipulation:

>   so, putting him to rage,
> You should have ta'en th'advantage of his choler,
> And passed him unelected.   (196ff)

'No one is immune to an ambush.' Whatever our previous view of the tribunes, here ethics and politics must clash. This kind of manipulation, taking advantage of a personal weakness, is like robbing a blind man. Yet in politics it is seldom that such a weakness fails to be exploited.

The first stage of the open confrontation between the tribunes and the people, on our left, and the patricians, on our right, a confrontation to be expressed in and through the person of Coriolanus, takes place in Act III, scene i. The whole sequence of political plot and counterplot has been set out so clearly by Shakespeare, individual and party perspectives defined so sharply, that we watch their interlocking with a sense of *déjà vu*. It is clear that the tribunes have the superior strategy and the more reliable actors. All that the patricians can do is nominate Coriolanus, hope that he will not anger the people, and trust that he will be elected. In the discussion that follows, although he takes the usual patrician attitude, with violent contempt for the people, Coriolanus—alone among his class—sees the absurdity of a situation in which the tribunes have power but no seat on the executive, while the senators supposedly have power but cannot control the tribunes (97ff). More important, he sees, almost for the first time, where a given pattern of action could lead to:

>   my soul aches
> To know, when two authorities are up,
> Neither supreme, how soon confusion

> May enter 'twixt the gap of both and take
> The one by th' other.   (III.i.108ff)

That is an impressive diagnosis of what social discord could do to Rome, and Shakespeare follows Plutarch in making Coriolanus the only man of the patrician class who has a grasp of the total political situation. (All that Cominius can do is to say, 'Well, on to th' market-place.') He sees, too, that the peculiarly vague distribution of power must mean that no government can continue: 'Purpose so barred, it follows / Nothing is done to purpose' (148f). Once again he is alone among the patricians in realizing that they are involved in a crucial power-struggle:

> Your dishonour
> Mangles true judgement and bereaves the state
> Of that integrity which should become't;
> Not having the power to do the good it would,
> For th'ill which doth control't.   (157ff)

Coriolanus is reaching political maturity fast. This is a penetrating series of comments on the current situation, the more praiseworthy given the silence of the rest of the patricians. Yet his remedies, as opposed to his diagnoses, are the old patrician extremist ones of more violence, starting with the abolition of the tribunes' office: 'at once pluck out / The multitudinous tongue', 'throw their power i'th'dust' (155f, 170). Openly challenged, the tribunes use their weapon against him by calling him a traitor (irony!) and calling for the aediles to arrest him. At this *'a rabble of Plebeians'* as Shakespeare's derogatory stage-direction has it, comes pouring in and *'all bustle about Coriolanus'*, while civil war seems to be at hand. As Menenius says: 'What is about to be? . . . Confusion's near' (188f). The civil violence implicit in the disorder becomes real when Coriolanus draws his sword and in the fighting (or *'this mutiny'*, as the stage-direction calls it) the tribunes, aediles and people are beaten away and the patricians hold the stage again. Coriolanus regards this as a military engagement: 'Stand fast; We have as many friends as enemies.' He has now, alas, no thought as to its future consequences for the state. It is left to Menenius to ask 'Shall it be put to that?'—'The gods forbid', a senator answers. Coriolanus having been the focus of all the violence so far, the patricians are relieved when they finally persuade him to go back to his house.

Coriolanus has left the stage but he is still the centre of discussion. The tribunes return, *'with the rabble again'*, and Menenius must somehow try to save the situation. The metaphors used by both sides are revealing. In contrast to Coriolanus' integrity and refusal to compromise, Menenius says that the rent in society 'must be patched / With cloth of any colour' (251f), and he tells Coriolanus that "tis a sore upon us / You cannot tent [heal] yourself' (234f). At this stage of Menenius' argument the 'sore' is something on society as a whole, distinct from Coriolanus: yet the metaphor of the body politic is a dangerous one to use, as we may have noticed from the silent transformations of the belly-fable—mostly damaging to the patricians—that have been going on since Menenius used it. Once under attack from the tribunes Menenius is forced to revise his metaphor:

> *Sicinius.* He's a disease that must be cut away.
> *Menenius.* O, he's a limb that has but a disease;
> Mortal, to cut it off; to cure it, easy.   (III.i.293ff)

On the defensive, Menenius concedes that Coriolanus *is* the sore, the centre of disease in the body politic. This is the first patrician betrayal of Coriolanus, for by conceding the tribunes' metaphor of him as the source of the disease in the body politic, they are powerless to argue against any extensions of that metaphor, such as Coriolanus as a 'gangrened' foot, which must be amputated to save the rest of the body, or as the source of a contagious disease (304ff). Faced with intolerance and violence, the patricians' only tactic seems to be to try and apply 'tact' and calmness, but to do so is futile, since they have lost the initiative and have no positive ideas to offer. In the end they merely concede their position to the tribunes. So proud and confident in advance of the election, they are now revealed as men of straw. All that Menenius manages to achieve is to have the tribunes drop the punishment of instant death and to allow Coriolanus to stand trial and 'answer, by a lawful form, / In peace, to his utmost peril' (322ff).

So far the power-conflict has been located in Coriolanus' struggle (along with the other patricians) against the plebeians. The women of the play have been absent from the political arena, as not having any right to be there. Now, however, sent off by the would-be placatory patricians, Coriolanus returns to his house, hoping to solve this crisis of behaviour in the political arena before he has to return to stand trial. When Volumnia appears he challenges her directly:

> I talk of you:
> Why did you wish me milder? would you have me

> False to my nature? Rather say I play
> The man I am.   (III.ii.13ff)

Whereas earlier he could only say, 'It is a part / That I shall blush in acting', now he has begun to realize that his embarrassment is a symptom of a deeper conflict: he now knows that his integrity is at stake. Shakespeare has controlled both the tempo and the level of the conflict during Act II so that Coriolanus has been confronted with relatively unproblematical issues. He was faced with a quick and urgent crisis that gave him no time to think of the issues involved: he had to act, and fell back on instinctively violent responses. The level at which the action existed was public rather than private, and the enemies were familiar ones, the people and their tribunes. Now, though, in his own house, away from the civil strife in the city, he is trying to understand the crisis, and turns to his mother for help. The problem he faces, without knowing it, is to find out how much his mother cares for him, whether she respects his integrity. This is in many ways the most decisive scene in the play.

His mother's first tactics are placatory, and Menenius even urges him to go back to the tribunes and 'repent' or withdraw what he has said; but Martius rejects this out of hand. Then Volumnia begins to give him a lesson in politics, starting, cleverly enough, with an argument from war:

> I have heard you say,
> Honour and policy, like unsevered friends,
> I'th'war do grow together.   (41ff)

We may doubt whether Coriolanus ever thought this—it sounds more like what she would say to him—for to Shakespeare and his contemporaries 'policy' carried all the overtones of deceit and manipulation. One could, however, accept that in a state of national emergency stratagems are permissible; yet Volumnia sees no difference between war and peace:

> If it be honour in your wars to seem
> The same you are not, which for your best ends
> You adopt your policy, how is it less or worse
> That it shall hold companionship in peace
> With honour as in war; since that to both
> It stands in like request?   (46ff)

The only proper reply to this suggestion is Cavour's famous remark: 'If we did for ourselves the things we do for Italy, what scoundrels we should be!' Everyone must recognize Volumnia's perversion of ethics: if one were to argue that for one's 'best ends', one's future advantage, any 'policy' is acceptable, then one would permit absolutely all forms of evil, violence, or destructiveness. Volumnia's appeal to naked self-interest is as degraded as the tribunes' readiness to preserve their power at whatever cost. (If she had been more subtle she would not have argued that the same behaviour is justified in peace as in war, but rather that Rome is at this present in a state of war.)

In her advice to 'seem the same you are not', Volumnia touches on the nerve-centre of Coriolanus' values. He has been told often enough by his class to dissimulate or conceal his real feelings about the people, now he is being urged to simulate affection for them, to effect a split between language and values. He should go to them not guided by his own feelings,

> Nor by th' matter which your heart prompts you,
> But with such words that are but roted in
> Your tongue, though but bastards and syllables
> Of no allowance to your bosom's truth. . . .   (53ff)

Volumnia recommends the separation between language and value, language and truth, with no compunction: it cannot 'dishonour' him to do this, and she herself would go much further:

> I would dissemble with my nature, where
> My fortunes and my friends at stake required
> I should do so in honour.   (62ff)

Having held the issue of integrity in reserve for so long Shakespeare now articulates it with the sharpest clarity. We know how antipathetic all this must be to Coriolanus, yet Volumnia seems neither to know nor care. The gap between them is greater than ever, and there can be no doubt as to which side has our sympathies. For Shakespeare not only articulates the issue but judges it. Volumnia is damned out of her own mouth by her corrupt advocacy of policy, by her sophistic and specious use of such words as 'honour' and 'truth', and by certain negative details of language. To call successful political words 'bastards' (illegitimate words, whose parentage one can disown without damaging one's 'bosom's truth'), is an attempt to devalue language which instead devalues her; and to offer to 'dissemble with my nature' is to make an extraordinarily unnatural effect. How could one do it?

Volumnia, however, has it all worked out. Coriolanus should go to the people, take his hat off to them, even kneel to them (for the Elizabethans two symbolic gestures for acknowledging the superiority of another party—one's parent, one's sovereign). He should beg their love, and feign love to them, a hypocritical procedure which she presents throughout in terms of the theatre (the word 'hypocrite' originally meant 'actor'), but which links up inescapably with the world of the politician. At this stage in our experience of this play there comes a tremendous shock as we realize that we have seen the hypocrite and the politician at work together earlier on: Volumnia's rehearsing of Coriolanus for a false political campaign is an exact parallel to the tribunes' rehearsal of the people. Both sides of society are using the same methods to gain political power. With great indignation Coriolanus agrees to go to the market-place:

> You have put me now to such a part which never
> I shall discharge to th' life.   (III.ii.104ff)

It is not in him to play this role. Coriolanus sees precisely what her dichotomy between language and truth will mean for him: his 'base tongue' will foist a lie on his 'noble heart', he will forfeit both integrity and authenticity.

Cominius offers—in a fine piece of linguistic irony—to 'prompt' Coriolanus, and Volumnia promises her son more maternal praise if he will 'perform a part / Thou hast not done before' (106ff). The theatrical analogy is becoming more insistent, and all the insulting implications of insincerity and deceit that have always been connected with the image of the actor well up into Coriolanus' great outburst:

> Well, I must do't.
> Away, my disposition, and possess me
> Some harlot's spirit! My throat of war be turned,
> Which choiréd with my drum, into a pipe
> Small as an eunuch or the virgin voice
> That babies lulls asleep! The smiles of knaves
> Tent in my cheeks, and schoolboys' tears take up
> The glasses of my sight! A beggar's tongue
> Make motion through my lips, and my armed knees,
> Who bowed but in my stirrup, bend like his
> That hath received an alms!   (III.ii.110ff)

This is one of the two most agonized speeches in the play (both come from Coriolanus), a series of images of perversion and travesty of the

REHEARSALS AND PERFORMANCE

self: in doing this he will be like a eunuch, a knave, a schoolboy, a beggar, all nauseating opposites to his true self. Most telling of all is the image of the beggar's tongue moving 'through' his lips, as if it were some other person's, or one manipulated by a puppeteer—but it would be his own. The level of feeling is so high that, confronted by this prefiguring of his imminent behaviour, Coriolanus breaks with it all:

> I will not do't;
> Lest I surcease to honour mine own truth,
> And by my body's action teach my mind
> A most inherent baseness. (120ff)

One can only admire Coriolanus at this point. Exposed for the first time to political manoeuvring, first in practice, now in theory, he sees with great force—with all the freshness of innocence—the extent of personal corruption involved in projecting a false political image. He is right, too, to see that the 'body's action' and the mind are organically related: debase one and you debase the other. Shakespeare has organized this ethical crisis in a deliberate, clear-cut intensity such as life seldom offers, for the emotional agony of Coriolanus derives from the realization, in pristine terms, of what we might call an absolute ethical concept: integrity is like virginity, you only have it once.

When Coriolanus began the scene by appealing to his conception of integrity Volumnia quickly deflected him to questions of power and dissimulation. Now that he has reached this absolute affirmation of integrity she can evidently no longer hope to sidetrack him. What she does is revelatory of the process by which she has so far trained and moulded him. To punish the recalcitrant child the mother withdraws her love, freezes him by isolation, works on his dependence on her until he is ready to abandon his own opinions and creep back into her approval and warmth (123ff). In the last few scenes Coriolanus has made an impressive breakthrough in his awareness of the nature of the political struggle in Rome and of the role that the patricians are expecting him to play in that struggle. We could have hoped that here he would be strong—or cold—enough to affirm his independence. But as Volumnia withdraws her love and projects her disapproval he cracks under it:

> Pray, be content:
> Mother, I am going to the market-place;
> Chide me no more. (130ff)

The humiliation of the last appeal ('please don't scold!') is pathetic, but at least as a chastised son Coriolanus realizes what the alternative for him now is:

> I'll mountebank their loves,
> Cog their hearts from them, . . . I'll return consul;
> Or never trust to what my tongue can do
> I'th'way of flattery further. (132ff)

The disgust in the verbs ('cog' and 'mountebank' are associated elsewhere in Shakespeare with 'policy' and similar processes of deceit) is now self-disgust, since Volumnia has left him no alternative. She has destroyed his integrity, pushed him back into the political arena where he can only be damaged further.

The confrontation in III.iii, when it finally takes place, fulfils our expectations with depressing accuracy. Shakespeare even prepares us for the event once more, although he has already written two long sequences in which the tribunes rehearsed the people. Leaving nothing to chance, they are at it again, manufacturing their image of him:

> *Brutus*. In this point charge him home, that he affects
> Tyrannical power. If he evade us there,
> Enforce him with his envy to the people,
> And that the spoil got on the Antiates
> Was ne'er distributed. (III.iii.1ff)

The people are again rehearsed in how to shout exactly what their leaders tell them to shout, 'either / For death, for fine, or banishment' (12ff).

The political behaviour being rehearsed once again is of the most loathsome kind, for, if their manipulation of the people should succeed, a newly-conceived democratic process will have given up its very identity, forfeited its integrity as a free and individual expression of opinion, and reduced itself to an indiscriminate support for any policy proposed by its leaders, however inhuman or arbitrary. It is as disgusting as Volumnia's advice to adopt any policy that serves 'Your best ends'. They repeat that the people must say whatever they are told to (19ff), and lay great stress on the need to make Coriolanus angry: once he speaks his mind he will break his neck (25ff). Credit must be given the tribunes for their political shrewdness ('know your enemy'), and for their careful preparation—what might be called today 'efficient campaigning'. (There seems hardly much point in stressing how eternally relevant this play is, when modern history offers us so many instances, from so many countries, of corrupt electioneering.)

The outcome is exactly according to the tribunes' plans. They call him a tyrant and a traitor, he erupts with anger (III.iii.68ff), and the well-drilled mob sentences him to be banished. The patricians have been routed, and Coriolanus' unwilling attempt to pervert his own integrity has failed; yet he is not defeated. This individual, expelled by society, replies:

> I banish you. . . . Despising
> For you the city, thus I turn my back:
> There is a world elsewhere.   (123, 133ff)

Some critics describe these words as arrogant, but it seems to me that in such a situation the individual is right to reject a corrupt society and to affirm the authenticity of his own values. As Coriolanus takes leave of Rome he compares his future existence to that of 'a lonely dragon that his fen / Makes feared and talked of more than seen' (IV.i.30f). The analogy with the dragon has been treated by some critics in the same way that they treat the references to Coriolanus as a fighting machine, that is, as if both represented criticisms of his inhumanity made by Shakespeare. What the image in fact means is that he is discouraging anyone from following or trying to approach him: the dragon is talked about rather than seen, since people are afraid to go near it. Just as society shuns the dragon, they have shunned him, and he will shun them. His intention is to isolate himself, and if he is an exceptionally strong—or cold—person then he might be able to sustain the isolation. Isolation exerts great pressures on a human being, and only those who are in an important sense self-sufficient can endure it.

4 Breaking Point

Rejected by Rome Coriolanus resolves to live outside society, a drastic transformation for any man. Yet he fails to do so, since he finds that he is not a dragon, that he needs human society and human action. After a short scene between a Roman and a Volsce (IV.iii.) which tells us that civil disorder is growing in Rome and that the patricians seem likely to follow Coriolanus' violent policies and deprive the tribunes of their power, we find Martius '*in mean apparel, disguised and muffled*' (IV.iv.s.d.), standing outside Aufidius' house. As he reflects on what it means for him to be in Antium we notice a quality of feeling in him which puts him apart from everyone else in the play, except Virgilia:

> A goodly city is this Antium. City,
> 'Tis I that made thy widows: many an heir
> Of these fair edifices 'fore my wars
> Have I heard groan and drop. (IV.iv.1ff)

This quality in Coriolanus, hardly commented on by any student of the play (an exception was the late Una Ellis-Fermor), is Coriolanus' sensitivity to the feelings, and especially the sufferings of others. No one else, Roman or Volscian—with the exception of Virgilia in her wifely love for him—evinces the slightest concern for the losses or sorrow of anyone other than themselves. Yet Shakespeare has shown his responsiveness in several places, such as his desire to repay the poor man in Corioli who needed his help and had once helped him (I.ix.82ff), or his deep sympathy for the women whose sons or husbands will not return from the war (II.i.173ff), or his attempt to soften his friends' suffering at the parting scene (IV.i.19ff).

The compassion and tenderness of Coriolanus represents a human value entirely absent from the Roman public world, as from his mother's attitude to him. The only other person in this world capable of experiencing or valuing such feelings is, significantly enough, Virgilia. If it is generally true that a man's choice of his wife reflects his own values found in her, or at least some of the attributes he values most, then Virgilia is an extension of Coriolanus' personality. With this as with other values Shakespeare stresses how Martius conflicts with the ethos of his class by constantly juxtaposing Virgilia and Volumnia, from their important first scene together (I.iii.) onwards. Virgilia's love is made by Shakespeare into a source of warmth and loyalty that is, however, felt rather than verbalized. She is the least articulate of all the major figures in the tragedies. This is in part due to the dominating presence of Volumnia, whose gigantic personality seems to reduce Virgilia to silence. But also, I think, it shows how out of place the tenderness of the Coriolanus-Virgilia relationship is in this ethos. Virgilia's characteristic utterance is a single sentence of exclamation for the safety or fortune of her husband, at the furthest remove from Volumnia's unfeeling gloating that 'he is wounded;

I thank the gods for't'. In contrast, Virgilia can only say, 'O, no, no, no.' (II.i.116ff). In the scene of parting Virgilia is made to speak twice only: 'O heavens! O heavens!' and 'O the gods!' is all that she can utter (IV.i.12, 37). This discrepancy between speech and feelings serves almost to increase our admiration for Virgilia, since so much of the language in this play is used to deceive and manipulate that at times we feel a certain distrust of language. Feeling not put into words can at least not be falsified.

Love outraged, denied its focus and fulfilment, can legitimately turn to hate. That is the experience of Virgilia (IV.ii.23ff), it is also the experience of Coriolanus. For in going to Antium he is not merely returning from the wilderness back to society but is instinctively looking for a way to revenge himself on Rome. The people of Rome repaid his service not with love but with ingratitude, and he will repay their hate not with love but with more hate. Some critics attack Coriolanus for wanting revenge on Rome, describing this as part of his colossal egoism. Perhaps on this issue modern critics should let themselves be guided by the view of that great exponent of the individual's contract with and debt to society, Thomas Hobbes. 'A man that by asperity of nature' will not cooperate with others, he declares, 'and for the stubbornness of his passions cannot be corrected, is to be left or cast out of society, as cumbersome thereunto' (*Leviathan*, I. 15; ed. W. Oakeshott (Oxford 1946) p. 99). Yet, once exiled, such a man no longer owes any services to his country:

For a banished man is a lawful enemy of the commonwealth that banished him; as being no more a member of the same. (II. 28; *ed. cit.*, p. 207)

After a sardonic scene with Aufidius' servants, who, like everyone else in this play, seize their chance to discuss Coriolanus and the political situation, Coriolanus finally comes face to face with his great rival Aufidius, and in a long speech (IV.v.68ff) offers his services in the destruction of Rome. Aufidius suppresses any resentment that he may feel about the past in his delight at having his most feared enemy transformed into an ally, and the atmosphere changes to one of harmony and cooperation. Yet no sooner have Aufidius and Coriolanus gone in to the banquet than the report by the servingmen of what took place there sows the first seeds of discord in this new alliance. At once Aufidius' prestige is reduced, since the Volscian leaders have divided his command with Coriolanus: 'the bottom of the news is, our general is cut i'th' middle, and but one half of what he was yesterday, for the other has half by the entreaty and grant of the whole table' (IV.v.202ff). Coriolanus' instant success with the Volscians is now presented as a threat to Aufidius' power, so motivating any jealousy or resentment from him.

In the sequence leading up to Act V, scene iii, the climax of the play, Shakespeare develops two dramatic movements which act, in effect, in opposed directions. From the perspective of Antium, Coriolanus' increasing success with the Volscian soldiers leads to jealousy, hatred, and a desire for revenge. These reactions (as usual hidden from the source and focus of them, Coriolanus himself) serve to undermine the general's apparent success, for Aufidius' envy takes the form of planning to allow Coriolanus to defeat Rome and then to destroy him:

> When, Caius, Rome is thine,
> Thou art poor'st of all; then shortly art thou mine. (IV.vii.56f)

In Aufidius' eyes, then, Coriolanus' future is limited, his present strength will be cut off once he has achieved a convenient task for the Volscians. But on either side of this scene Shakespeare gives us the perspective of Rome, in which Coriolanus' strength seems enormous and threatening. The second view is of course correct, since Aufidius will wait until after the victory before taking his revenge. The two perspectives offer us, in effect, a scale of power of descending magnitude, which, using the symbol >('greater than') can be set out as: Aufidius > Coriolanus > Rome. If we think back to the beginning of the play we will remember that the power-structure then was just the reverse: Rome > Coriolanus >Aufidius. In a number of details the final stages of the play reverse the initial ones, as we will see if we think for a moment in terms of such general concepts involved in much human action as the Pressurizer (or influencer); the agent; the goal; and the obstacles to achieving that goal. The play has, so far as we can see at the moment, three movements, War (Acts I–II); Politics (Acts II–IV); and Revenge (Acts IV–V). Set out as a diagram the following structure can be seen:

Stage	Pressurizer	Agent	Goal	Obstacles	Outcome
I	Rome	Coriolanus	Defeat Aufidius	The citizens	Success
II	Volumnia and patricians	Coriolanus	Gain consulship	Tribunes and citizens	Failure
III	Aufidius	Coriolanus	Defeat Rome	Volumnia and patricians	

In all three movements so far Coriolanus is pressurized, acted upon ('put upon') in order to act. Individuals and groups use him to effect their own

ends, and in each case he could say, as he says to the soldiers who take him
as their leader against Corioli, 'Make you a sword of me?' (I.vi.76). But
although the pressurizer and goal have become interchanged from stage I
to stage III the situation is still the same in that Coriolanus is being
manipulated without realizing it. He is always the agent, willing or
unwilling, knowing or unknowing.

To the Romans, however, all this is as obscure as it is to him. Writing
with undiminished fullness and energy at the end of what has already
been a long and dense play, Shakespeare develops the perspective of
Rome in full detail. In doing so he not only shows their present situation,
but sheds fresh light on the events of the past. When the news of
Coriolanus' march on Rome is confirmed the tribunes collapse abjectly,
denying that they were responsible for his banishment. Yet Menenius, in
attacking them, also indicts the patricians:

> We loved him, but, like beasts
> And cowardly nobles, gave way unto your clusters,
> Who did hoot him out o'th'city.   (IV.vi.122ff)

So Coriolanus' complaint that he has been betrayed by the patricians is
validated. They would not risk their own skin but gladly sacrificed their
candidate, and in this respect the aristocracy were just as monstrous as the
people.

Rome seems on the verge of destruction. The patricians do what they
can to save it, and in a sequence of scenes each of the major characters goes
in turn to Coriolanus as a suppliant. We learn about Cominius' embassy
after the event, as, unsuccessful, he explains to Menenius and the tribunes
how coldly he was treated, he who 'was sometime his general, who loved
him/In a most dear particular' (V.i.2f). Coriolanus did not seem even to
know Cominius, and dismissed him with no sympathy. Menenius'
supplication (V.ii) is both comic and pathetic. To begin with he cannot
even get past the watchmen, under orders to admit no one from Rome. In
order to impress them, Menenius describes his past relationship with
Coriolanus, and in so doing Shakespeare makes him illuminate
retrospectively the whole rationale of the patricians' representation of
Coriolanus, the sequence that I have described as <action : evaluation :
report : adulation : advantage>. Here the truth behind the image-making
finally appears:

> I tell thee, fellow,
> Thy general is my lover. I have been

The book of his good acts whence men have read
His fame unparalleled—haply amplified;
For I have ever varnishéd my friends
(Of whom he's chief) with all the size that verity
Would without lapsing suffer: nay, sometimes,
Like to a bowl upon a subtle ground,
I have tumbled past the throw, and in his praise
Have almost stamped the leasing: . . .   (V.ii.14ff)

This is an astonishingly revealing speech, which seems to have no immediate dramatic function. Indeed its central human relationship is obsolete, for there can be no future for Menenius as a panegyrist for Coriolanus. Perhaps he thinks that Coriolanus owes him a debt of gratitude for all his efforts in compiling 'the book of his good acts'—but Coriolanus never wanted them. The actual function of the speech seems to be to recall how the patricians acted as if they owned Coriolanus, as if he represented, in the language of Hollywood, a 'property' (a word that is applied both to a performer and a script), a property that becomes more valuable the more it is celebrated. Menenius confesses that he may have amplified him too much but that in general he 'laid on as much praise as would stick', but without 'verity' suffering a lapse. Yet, to be perfectly honest (damaging to him though that will be), and using a self-excusing metaphor from bowls, in the exercise of panegyric he has sometimes inadvertently gone too far and given falsehood the stamp of truth (19ff). So, Menenius claims, he has a right to pass. The soldiers substitute for Menenius' euphemisms a frank description which echoes Coriolanus' own (I.ix.50ff): Menenius has uttered 'lies in his behalf', has been not the general's 'lover' but his 'liar'—as if that were a permanent office, such as cup-bearer or treasurer. (Under the later Roman emperors panegyrists were indeed employed full-time and enjoyed great status and vast rewards, rather like a modern promotion or advertising agency.)

Despite the watchmen's efforts the meeting takes place, and we observe with embarrassment how Menenius becomes cloyingly sentimental, weeping with joy, affirming that the gods 'love thee no worse than thy old father Menenius does! O my son, my son!' (66ff)—and so on in a fast and incoherent prose speech. All the more cutting, then, is Coriolanus' reply, stylistically distanced by being in verse:

> *Coriolanus.* Away!
> *Menenius.* How! away!
> *Coriolanus.* Wife, mother, child, I know not. My affairs

> Are servanted to others. Though I owe
> My revenge properly, my remission lies
> In Volscian breasts. (77ff)

That is, his revenge is his own, but the power to pardon belongs entirely to the Volscians. For him, Shakespeare reminds us again, pardon is impossible since his natural pity has been killed by Rome's ungrateful forgetting of his services to them (82ff).

At this stage Coriolanus seems completely in control of himself and others. Yet he has just made a mistake. He thinks that it was Rome's 'latest refuge', or last resort, to send Menenius, but in the last scene but one Shakespeare alerted us, through Cominius, that Rome's last hope consists of

> his noble mother, and his wife—
> Who, as I hear, mean to solicit him
> For mercy to his country. (V.i.71ff)

Rome hangs on this thread, and so does Coriolanus. For across the apparently final sequence of the play, Aufidius' move against Rome, Shakespeare has spaced out three contrasting counter-moves:

Stage	Pressurizer	Agent	Goal	Obstacle	Outcome
III	Aufidius	Coriolanus	Defeat Rome	Volumnia and patricians	
IIIa	Rome	Cominius	Spare Rome	Coriolanus	Failure
IIIb	Rome	Menenius	Spare Rome	Coriolanus	Failure
IIIc	Rome	Volumnia, Virgilia, young Martius	Spare Rome	Coriolanus	

These three counter-moves are treated contrastingly, too, in ascending order of proximity to Coriolanus. We heard about Cominius' encounter only after the event, and by a report; we saw Menenius and Coriolanus face to face; and finally Coriolanus is not only confronted immediately by his family but is given a long aside, a virtual soliloquy, to tell us directly what he is feeling. We come closer to him, as he to them.

Coriolanus hears shouting. He does not know who is coming but, curiously enough, anticipates that he is about to be put under pressure.

> Shall I be tempted to infringe my vow
> In the same time 'tis made? I will not. (V.iii.20f)

He needs to stiffen himself already. Hard and inflexible as he has been to
the patricians, he is now exposed to his whole family, dressed in
mourning. He has perhaps dismissed the possibility of their intercession
because on the Roman political stage women have played no part. Now
they approach him, as he sits in a chair of state—with Aufidius standing
by him, and for 16 lines we see through his eyes and feelings what they
mean to him.

> My wife comes foremost; then the honoured mould
> Wherein this trunk was framed, and in her hand
> The grandchild to her blood. But out, affection!
> All bond and privilege of nature, break!
> Let it be virtuous to be obstinate.   (22ff)

He acts as a quasi-neutral commentator describing their arrival, yet his
personal feelings keep breaking through. He records their impression on
him and at once fights against it, denying his love. He attempts a
perversion of himself, and in the language Shakespeare gives him we see
him making an effort to reject his fundamental nature which, were it to
succeed, would be just as unnatural as if he were to try to fawn, flatter and
dissemble. Words like 'affection', 'nature' and 'virtuous' cannot be
deprived of their positive, creative connotations, at least not by someone
as patently natural and lacking in guile as Coriolanus.

The great paradox of this scene is the struggle within Coriolanus and
the consequent split in the reader's or spectator's sympathies. He is trying
to be hard-hearted, so that he can go through with his revenge on Rome.
Since he has our sympathies for the way in which the Romans have
treated him we might want him to succeed in this revenge. Yet our wish
for revenge is confronted with all those feelings of love and tenderness
towards those closest to him that have been so impressive throughout the
play. (To speak personally, I cannot wish him to close up and deny those
feelings. I would rather he expressed them, even though it may mean his
death.) He had meant to remain seated, distanced from all the suppliants
by his formal position in his chair of state. Yet the pressure of feeling is so
great that he realizes that this is another unnatural role that he simply
cannot sustain. He has to go to Virgilia:

> [rising]. Like a dull actor now
> I have forgot my part and I am out,
> Even to a full disgrace. [goes to her] Best of my flesh,
> Forgive my tyranny; but do not say,

For that, 'Forgive our Romans.' O, a kiss
Long as my exile, sweet as my revenge!   (41ff)

He welcomes his mother with great reverence, acknowledging his inferiority to her (like a molehill to Olympus, as he puts it) and kneels down before her. From this point on Volumnia dominates the scene, both as producer and as chief actor.

In a sense this scene defies criticism. Shakespeare has built everything up towards this point, has made the forces of pressure so clear that the collision between them becomes totally explicit. The scene does not need to be explicated: it needs to be felt.

Coriolanus tries to prohibit them from making any requests on him (82ff), but Volumnia will not be deterred, and forces him to allow her to supplicate. At this point the scene is transformed from a private back into a public action. Coriolanus sits on his throne of state again and bids Aufidius and the Volsces to observe his behaviour: 'mark', he says (92), as if confident of giving a demonstration of a strong and cold man rejecting attempts to weaken his will. Volumnia's first speech (of 30 lines) is a carefully structured piece of rhetoric, beginning by describing their costume, drawing attention to his family's rags and emaciated condition, juxtaposing their present state of 'fear and sorrow' with their normal feelings in the past on being reunited with him, when their eyes would 'flow with joy, hearts dance with comforts' (94ff). Her most important tactic is to stress the triple relationship that binds Coriolanus, as Shakespeare makes still more clear by putting it into correlative verse:

Making the mother, wife, and child, to see
The son, the husband, and the father, tearing
His country's bowels out.   (101ff)

Coriolanus had always rejected the idea that he could play an unnatural role, so it is ironic that he should now be trapped by the three natural roles that he cannot help playing. Having started with her main claim on him Volumnia now shifts to the claims of the state, ringing the changes, with much elaborate rhetorical parallelism, on their dilemma of having to pray both for their country and for his person (106ff). She claims that he can hardly destroy the city without also shedding his 'wife and children's blood' (116ff). Characteristically, Volumnia seizes that point to exert all possible pressure, and in so doing produces one of the most tragic moments in the play:

> *Volumnia.*   . . . thou shalt no sooner
> March to assault thy country than to tread—
> Trust to't, thou shalt not—on thy mother's womb,
> That brought thee to this world.
> *Virgilia.*   Ay, and mine,
> That brought you forth this boy, to keep your name
> Living to time.   (122ff)

It is only to be expected that Volumnia will use the most emotive weapons possible. As with 'tearing his country's bowels out' earlier, she goes straight for the soft middle of the body, using a rhetoric calculated to make the enemy seem a monster and a pervert: this is another belly fable. But it is a terrible moment when Virgilia follows Volumnia's cue, when she betrays her husband and sides with the values of the patrician class. This is the last time that she speaks to him in the play, an awful note for their relationship to end on.

Stung by these pressures Coriolanus tries to escape from the situation by ending the interview, getting down from his throne to symbolize that the audience is over:

> Not of a woman's tenderness to be,
> Requires nor child nor woman's face to see.
> I have sat too long.   [*rising*.   (129ff)

Yet this, too, is a futile attempt to deny his own nature, that tenderness that is not womanish but essentially human. Undeterred, Volumnia continues with more arguments, and as he remains silent she urges him to speak: 'speak to me, son' (148), she says, invoking natural relationships only so that he will give in to her, 'Why dost not speak?' (153). She knows that 'His heart's his mouth: / What his breast forges, that his tongue must vent' (III.i.256f), and that if he can be brought to speak then he will give way. So she urges Virgilia and young Martius to speak:

> Daughter, speak you:
> He cares not for your weeping. Speak thou, boy: . . . (155f)

But important as those relationships are to Coriolanus they are relationships of love, not power. They cannot be made to bend or break him, since they would first break themselves. Volumnia is the only one with the big pull, and she exerts it.

There's no man in the world
More bound to's mother, yet here he lets me prate
Like one i' th' stocks. Thou hast never in thy life
Showed the dear mother any courtesy. . . .   (V.iii.158ff)

Surprisingly to her, perhaps, he still hasn't given in; but he *'turns away'*, which might mean that he is wavering, or trying to hide his feelings. So she stage-manages another use of gesture as pressure:

> Down, ladies; let us shame him with our knees.
> To his surname Coriolanus 'longs more pride
> Than pity to our prayers. Down: an end;
> [*The four all kneel*   (169ff)

Yet even this gesture fails, he does not raise them up or relent. Volumnia's failure, though, means that she and her fellow-actors have to go through the indignity of standing up again, and as they prepare to leave in defeat she throws her last weapon:

> Come, let us go: [*They rise*
> This fellow had a Volscian to his mother;
> His wife is in Corioli, and his child
> Like him by chance.   (177ff)

Here Volumnia plays her last card, that withdrawal of a mother's love which had worked so well in the past. But here she even cancels her relationship with him, disowns him and thus denies 'nature' and 'affection'. Coriolanus had attempted to deny these concepts earlier, in the long soliloquy as his family had approached, but he had failed: Volumnia succeeds. In his mouth words such as 'affection' or 'nature' refused to take on a sophistic sense, rebounded rather as the fixed points by which his attempted alternatives were tested and found lacking:

> my young boy
> Hath an aspect of intercession which
> Great Nature cries 'Deny not.' Let the Volsces
> Plough Rome, and harrow Italy: I'll never
> Be such a gosling to obey instinct, but stand
> As if a man were author of himself
> And knew no other kin.   (V.iii.31ff)

'Stand' he has done, throughout this scene, attempting to 'stick i'th'wars / Like a great sea-mark', withstanding every pressure. Yet the whole

attempt to 'stand', in this context, is a perversion, against which 'Great
Nature cries "Deny not",' for 'instinct' knows that a man is not author of
himself, cannot be 'a lonely dragon'. When Volumnia disclaims him,
then, denies the 'bond and privilege of nature', it seems finally to snap
Coriolanus' denial, it changes him from a man who stands alone to one
who puts out his hand, in acknowledgment of nature and relationship. In
one of the most poignantly expressive stage-directions in all drama, he
Holds her by the hand silent. (V.iii.183). It is the moment of victory for her,
defeat for him. And for once he seems to know it:

> O mother, mother!
> What have you done? Behold, the heavens do ope,
> The gods look down, and this unnatural scene
> They laugh at. O my mother, mother! O!
> You have won a happy victory to Rome;
> But, for your son—believe it, O, believe it—
> Most dangerously you have with him prevailed,
> If not most mortal to him.   (182ff)

The laughter of the gods, beholding the follies of man on the stage of the
theatrum mundi, is a finely ironic summation of the theatrical nature of this
scene, the costume, tableau, gestures and speeches of which were all
controlled by Volumnia. For a moment Coriolanus speaks with his old
bitterness to her as he regards this 'unnatural scene', on which his mother
has played the most unnatural role. But feelings of waste and regret
dominate him, as they must us.

Since the pressure has broken his attempt to play an unnatural role, has
shown him to be fundamentally true to his private world, he can now
only be false to his public one and to 'good Aufidius', as he calls him
rather entreatingly. Announcing that he intends to make peace he appeals
to his new colleague to understand, and forgive, his collapse into feeling
(191ff). Aufidius is noncommittal, but gives his real reaction to the scene
in an aside to us, another crucial utterance that takes place behind
Coriolanus' back:

> I am glad thou hast set thy mercy and thy honour
> At difference in thee. Out of that I'll work
> Myself a former fortune.   (200ff)

The collapse or 'melting' of Coriolanus' honour to his pity is action in the
present which will have great future advantage for Volumnia, for the
patricians, and for Rome in general; it will also be of great benefit to

Aufidius, who can now manipulate Coriolanus in such a way as to regain his 'former fortune', all his earlier prestige. Everyone benefits, then, except Coriolanus. From being the agent in the assault of Aufidius on Rome Coriolanus has been transformed, by the successful supplication of Volumnia, into the obstacle that frustrated that assault. He has been pressurized, once again, turned from an active to a passive role, his will and desires smashed by his own mother, acting on behalf of his own class.

5 Death of a Puppet

Having presented the events leading up to his climax from the twin perspectives of Antium and Rome, Shakespeare, not skimping in either length or detail, deals with the after-effects of the climax from both points of view. The confrontation took place at the tent of Coriolanus, in the Volscian camp outside Rome, from which Menenius had been dismissed in the scene before. When the scene shifts back to Rome, therefore, it is just in time to find Menenius meeting Sicinius and telling him the outcome of the embassy which the tribunes had entreated him to perform (V.i.39ff, 47ff, 59ff). Since Menenius was dismissed from Coriolanus' tent before the women reached there he does not know the result of their embassy. News travels slowly for the people of Rome, but more quickly for the spectators of the play, who realize that the situation Menenius is about to describe is already out of date. Menenius is not cast down by his news but positively exults in the approaching destruction, since the tribunes were responsible for it. The terms in which he reports his interview will remind us of other passages in the play:

Menenius. . . . This Martius is grown from man to dragon: he has wings; he's more than a creeping thing.
Sincinius. He loved his mother dearly.
Menenius. So did he me: and he no more remembers his mother now than an eight-year-old horse. The tartness of his face sours ripe grapes; when he walks, he moves like an engine and the ground shrinks before his treading. He is able to pierce a corslet with his eye, talks like a knell, and his hum is a battery. He sits in his state as a thing made for Alexander.

What he bids be done is finished with his bidding. He wants nothing of a god but eternity and a heaven to throne in. (V.iv.12ff)

There are all the familiar processes of the patricians' propaganda for Coriolanus, turning him into a colossus, a war-machine with an eye like a laser-beam, a 'hum' like the noise of an artillery battery, his gait like a battering-ram. Once again he is made into an image of unnature or anti-nature: his face sours grapes, his speech is a 'knell'—the sound of a bell at a funeral—the ground shrinks before him, 'there is no more mercy in him than there is milk in a male tiger' (27f). Yet, as everyone must now see, these are more false images created for a deterrent effect, increasingly improbable analogies for this man whom we have just seen break down and weep, 'melt', his 'honour' drowned by the flow of his 'mercy' and 'pity'. The last ironic comment on their tactics of over-inflated report ('varnished' up to the maximum, we remember), is Sicinius' rejoinder: 'Yes, mercy, if you report him truly.' Menenius claims, 'I paint him in the character' (25f) but is soon proved totally, comprehensively wrong by the return of the women bringing peace and 'love'.

From triumph in Rome we move to conspiracy in Corioli, with Aufidius delivering an indictment of Coriolanus to the nobles and anticipating how his enemy

> Intends t'appear before the people, hoping
> To purge himself with words.   (V.vi.5ff)

There is yet another reversal accomplished by these closing stages, now of everything that Coriolanus has stood for. He no longer has deeds to offer but only words, and those false ones. But his behaviour is being observed and predicted, once again, as a new group of people, Aufidius with '*three or four Conspirators*', construct a scenario in which Coriolanus is again to play the central and pressurized role. Here, too, the manipulators pretend to respect the mind of 'the people', but conclude that they will be so indiscriminate or fickle as to follow whichever faction destroys the other. All that is now lacking is a party manifesto, and Aufidius promptly produces one, in which Coriolanus is presented as a hypocrite and a flatterer who had seduced Aufidius' friends away from him (21ff). The picture is so amazingly false that one of Aufidius' own supporters is moved to protest, recalling 'his stoutness / When he did stand for consul, which he lost / By lack of stooping' (27ff). That, however, is no longer part of official history. We see that this anti-Coriolanus party, like the others, is creating an image of him for their own purposes. To the patricians a depersonalized fighting machine, to the tribunes arrogant and ambitious, to Volumnia proud and ungrateful, to Aufidius and his supporters he is now a corrupt flatterer. And, as with the other enemies of Coriolanus, Shakespeare makes it perfectly clear that what is driving their manipulation of him is their own self-interest:

> *Aufidius.* . . . At a few drops of women's rheum, which are
> As cheap as lies, he sold the blood and labour
> Of our great action: therefore shall he die,
> And I'll renew me in his fall.   (46ff)

Wherever he turns Coriolanus seems to be either the agent in one group's plot or the obstacle in the way of some other group. All the political and personal pressures of the play meet in him.

For what seems like the umpteenth time, Coriolanus enters on to a scene in complete ignorance of the plot which we have seen hatched to manipulate him. One other lie that the conspirators attempt to plant is that Martius threw away the whole cost of raising the army and brought the Volsces nothing in return (64ff). This economic aspect of war is one that has never appealed to him (we recall that Cominius shrewdly offered his soldiers the spoils of battle as incentive, but that Coriolanus offered service and self-sacrifice), so it comes as a surprise to us when Coriolanus answers the lie by stating that his audited accounts declare a more than 30 per cent profit; it is also a surprise to find him praising his own achievements. At last he sounds like the conquering hero or politic soldier:

> Hail, lords! I am returned your soldier;
> No more infected with my country's love
> Than when I parted hence, but still subsisting
> Under your great command. You are to know
> That prosperously I have attempted, and
> With bloody passage led your wars even to
> The gates of Rome. Our spoils we have brought home
> Doth more than counterpoise a full third part
> The charges of the action. We have made peace
> With no less honour to the Antiates
> Than shame to th' Romans; . . .   (71ff)

The style of that speech would bear detailed comparison with the vauntings of Cominius in Act II, with its abrupt and assertive rhythms, its self-confident proclamatory syntax, its generalissimo's plural, its formalized inversions ('prosperously I have attempted', 'With bloody passage led'). More important than the style is our discovery that, like other successful soldiers, Coriolanus has finally learned the trick of presenting his actions in a more favourable light than they actually deserve. He did not capture the city: true, but he led his army 'even to / The gates of Rome'; he did not defeat the Romans: true, but he made a peace with 'shame' to them. . . . He makes his failures look like successes, a very useful ability in a general.

But it is an accomplishment that debases him, and we are almost relieved that he has learned it too late. For Aufidius' attack on him, Shakespeare writes a speech with all his astonishing skill in projecting himself into individual human perspectives, a speech that presents the whole of the suppliant scene in the most distorted and malicious light imaginable:

> He has betrayed your business and given up,
> For certain drops of salt, your city Rome,
> I say 'your city', to his wife and mother;
> Breaking his oath and resolution, like
> A twist of rotten silk; never admitting
> Counsel o' th' war; but at his nurse's tears
> He whined and roared away your victory;
> That pages blushed at him and men of heart
> Looked wond'ring each at other.   (92ff)

Having seen the original action that is now reported and evaluated here, we can appreciate the brilliant ingenuity of the distortion; yet we have to admit the underlying truths, that he did give up Rome to his 'wife and mother', that he did break his 'oath and resolution', that he did not take 'counsel' from his fellow officers. But none of these, perhaps, is as painful as the final shameful image of a man whining and blubbering so much that boys are made to blush (blushing is Coriolanus' own instinctive reaction to embarrassment). Now, if Coriolanus had learned anything from his confrontation with the tribunes, he might think 'Ah, yes, that's just what I expected him to do: he's trying to provoke me, but I shan't let him, for I can see where all this is leading.' However, still innocent of the future, evaluating action and speech for what they represent when performed, he bursts under this pressure on his honour:—'Hear'st thou, Mars?'—an exclamation that Aufidius seizes on for the most cutting insult yet: 'Name not the god, thou boy of tears!' (100f).

When Coriolanus had reviewed the types of self-perversion which he would suffer by fawning to the mob they included that in which 'schoolboys' tears take up / The glasses of my sight!' (III.ii.116f). Having created his hero Shakespeare knows just how to hurt him most, and at this provocation his real nature asserts itself, no longer dressing up words to disguise the deeds recorded by them but speaking what he feels:

> Measureless liar, thou hast made my heart
> Too great for what contains it. (103f)

He can neither dissemble nor repress his natural, instinctual feelings for long: out they must come, directly. This was the great redeeming factor in the suppliant scene, and it is the quality that his enemies can always exploit to destroy him. Faced with a distortion of his true 'report', which is as extreme as either the under-valuation of the tribunes or the over-valuation of the patricians, Coriolanus—like Othello at the last moment of his tragedy—affirms his true worth and report:

> 'Boy'! False hound!
> If you have writ your annals true, 'tis there,
> That, like an eagle in a dove-cote, I
> Fluttered your Volscians in Corioli.
> Alone I did it. 'Boy!' (113ff)

And as with Othello, the hero has to make his own self-validation because no one else will do it for him: those who love him are absent or dead. Both tragic heroes reach their greatness again, but both do so only by retrospective narration, and only for a moment. Despite the protests of one of the Volscian lords, who wishes Coriolanus to have a judicial hearing (126f), the conspirators, egged on by the insults of Aufidius ('unholy braggart', 'Insolent villain'), descend on him with the mob's shout: 'Kill, kill, kill, kill, kill him!' In a play remarkable for graphic and explicit authorial stage-directions the instructions to the actors here sum up Coriolanus' final reversal:

> Draw all the Conspirators, and kill Martius, who falles.
> Aufidius stands on him.

Not only does that deed project Coriolanus all the way down from his first moment of greatness in Corioli to his last indignity—once again he is the only Roman in the city—but it catches up and reverses the terms of Volumnia's bloodthirsty prediction:

> He'll beat Aufidius' head below his knee,
> And tread upon his neck.   (I.iii.47f)

This whole sequence creates in us, once more, that feeling of predictability. Yet again a conspiratorial plot has succeeded in dislodging Coriolanus. He has not learned—but then he has not had much time to learn, and he has no one to teach him. The coaching by the patricians on the presentation of the self have been oddly lacking in instruction on how to avoid being manipulated by others.

What is new about this scene is that the enemies of Coriolanus not only express their hatred openly, but follow it with apparent regret. Aufidius falsely claims that Coriolanus offered a great threat to the Volscian state, and one of the lords excuses Aufidius' 'impatience' on these grounds. Then the chief villian of the scene leaves with a closing speech, the apparently conventional epitaph on a dead hero, which is so remarkable as to deserve quoting in full:

> *Aufidius.*   My rage is gone,
> And I am struck with sorrow. Take him up:
> Help, three o'th' chiefest soldiers; I'll be one.
> Beat thou the drum, that it speak mournfully:
> Trail your steel pikes. Though in this city he
> Hath widowed and unchilded many a one,
> Which to this hour bewail the injury,
> Yet he shall have a noble memory.
> Assist.
>
> *Exeunt bearing the Body of Martius.*
> *A dead March Sounded.*   (147ff)

Setting aside the military details we have here an utterly unconvincing *volte-face* from Aufidius, who changes from 'rage' to 'sorrow' in the twinkling of an eye, 'before a man can say "one"'. The new mood that he establishes so quickly silences further discussion, for the ritual must proceed, and the appropriate noises of eulogy can be made. One critic who noticed the injustice of this sequence was John Dennis, writing in 1711. He protested that just as Sicinius and Brutus had been guilty of a notorious injustice (in getting 'the Champion and Defender of their Country banish'd upon a pretended Jealousy', out of 'Hatred and Malice') yet remained 'unpunish'd', so Aufidius, 'the principal Murderer of Coriolanus, who in cold Blood gets him assassinated by Ruffians instead of leaving him to the Law of the Country and the Justice of the

Volscian Senate, and who commits so black a Crime not by any erroneous Zeal or a mistaken Publick Spirit but thro' Jealousy, Envy, and inveterate Malice; this Assassinator not only survives, and survives unpunish'd, but seems to be rewarded for so detestable an Action by engrossing all those Honours to himself which Coriolanus before had shar'd with him' (Dennis, pp. 284f). To Dennis this was evidence that Shakespeare failed his duty of writing according to poetic justice; to us, however, the ending is proof rather of a deeper irony, familiar from contemporary history. It is all so demonstrably false that the appropriate comparison would be from modern totalitarian states: when a particularly awkward enemy has been disposed of, nothing is more effective than to give him a state funeral and a memorial, build up a legend, make him seem missed. To do so cannot harm you, indeed the generosity you thus display may even work to your future advantage.

6 Success in Failure

The ending of Coriolanus is ironic not only in its hollow and false epitaph, and not only in the mechanical way in which Martius, puppet-man, is manipulated once more for someone else's benefit. It is ironic in relation to the rest of the play, and to the political and family situation in Rome. All the other Shakespearian tragedies similarly witness the death of the greatest, most outstanding people, yet they do effect a change in an unsatisfactory political situation; they leave some lesser but nonetheless reliable person in charge of a new set-up, in which order rules and from which the destructive influences have been purged. Fortinbras rules at the end of Hamlet, Edgar in King Lear, Malcolm in Macbeth, Octavius in Antony and Cleopatra, Alcibiades in Timon, even Cassio takes charge of Cyprus in Othello. Yet in Coriolanus the hero dies while nothing else has changed. Brutus and Sicinius, despite the patricians' threats, are still tribunes, and can be relied on to foment class-hatred in future. Menenius will still try to fob the people off with his image of the bluff but friendly aristocrat. Volumnia, given increased prestige by the monument erected to her, will still incarnate the militarist fantasy, while Virgilia will be as

Tom222

loving and as ineffectual as ever. And the warrior of the future?—that will be little Martius, already under his grandmother's influence.

As a reader not normally given to speculation about what happens after the ending of a Shakespeare play, or indeed any other literary work, I can perhaps defend myself here by pointing to the unique qualities of *Coriolanus*. No other Shakespeare play offers so penetrating and so sustained an analysis of political processes, from image-making and vote-catching to the cut-and-thrust of an election and the cloak-and-dagger work of a conspiracy eliminating political enemies. No other Shakespeare play is so critical of practically all the characters involved in it: the people, the tribunes, the patricians, Volumnia, Aufidius—it is difficult to find anything favourable to say or feel about any of these, and if we put Coriolanus and Virgilia in a separate category then we still have reservations about them. Taking these two factors together, then, the disillusioned analysis of political processes with all the malice and distortion they involve, and the relentlessly scathing examination of personality and motive, I would suggest that the open, unresolved ending of the play is Shakespeare's final irony about politics. The innocent and unwary perish, but the party machines grind on: the faces may be different next time but the pressures will be the same, the compromises and dissimulations will still work to weaken and distort truth and honesty. Democratic processes will still be open to exploitation; the people will always believe that image which is most cleverly constructed, not that which is true, but less attractive. Of course, exponents of Shakespeare the pure artist, unconcerned with life, will protest at this suggestion, as will defenders of politics as an arena of sweetness and light. But one thing is clear about *Coriolanus*, and that is that its criticism of political manœuvring cannot be laughed off. One exposure to the play should be enough to destroy our complacency about politics for ever.

It is a marvellously critical and polemical work, then—but is it a tragedy? Criteria for tragedy are not generally agreed on, yet a minimal definition might be that in this genre unavoidable human conflict results in the destruction of important values, an eclipse of people and relationships which moves us with sorrow and pity for all this loss and unfulfilment. Here the major tragic experience is the betrayal of Coriolanus by the people of Rome, by the tribunes, by his mother, by his class, by Aufidius, and, unless I am mistaken (I hope I am), by his wife. Although often unaware of the real forces acting on him Coriolanus struggles from first to last to maintain his own integrity and identity, to remain true to his own values. The many points during the action where he can be found indignantly protesting at the violation of some basic principle shows that he not only lives his values but feels them, and feels them at maximum intensity always. He is never cool, detached, or indifferent about his beliefs.

As a system of values I have already indicated where I take it to be deficient, notably in its contempt for the people. Yet Shakespeare, deliberately retaining this unsympathetic trait, has gone to even greater pains to show that Coriolanus has taken over—or rather, been indoctrinated into—an attitude deriving from the whole patrician class. On the other side he shows the people as being contemptible in every way, and judged so by their own leaders. Nonetheless it is an unsympathetic trait, and in the first two Acts it serves to restrain us from becoming involved with Coriolanus. This calculatedly unfavourable first impression is one that Shakespeare uses for other tragic characters—Lear, Antony, Timon—but in each case he creates a far greater final involvement than if the characters had been admirable from the first. The turning-point in our attitude to Coriolanus comes in Act III, scene i, the great confrontation between patricians and plebeians in which Coriolanus alone sees the tribunes' plot and the consequences for society of this unresolvable division of power. In that and in subsequent scenes (as indeed in the battle in Act I) the people and their leaders are shown to be as bad as Coriolanus says they are, while the patricians are shown to be as ineffectual as he says they are (III.i.91ff). As the action develops from this point Coriolanus' unsympathetic qualities are played down by Shakespeare, they recede into the past with the Roman situation from which he has been expelled. In the second half of the play, it seems to me, Coriolanus is never criticized by Shakespeare: we are meant always to approve of him.

Yet, clearly, we do not approve of him in the abstract or in a vacuum. The special quality of human behaviour in mimetic forms such as the novel and drama is that in our experience of it we evaluate men and women partly through their own actions and partly by comparison with others. Coriolanus' character is presented to us in enough detail for us to form a full impression of it, yet it is defined even more sharply by its contrast with other people. These juxtapositions are made between him and everyone else, starting, as we have observed, with the gap between his attitude to love and relationship and that of Volumnia. His modesty and loathing of panegyrical lies is reiterated by Shakespeare through the contrast with Cominius and Menenius, a contrast that extends from the first Act to the last. His dedication to war as an image of service to the state is juxtaposed with the worship of blood and death expressed by Volumnia and Menenius and with the craven and self-seeking behaviour of the citizens. His honesty in expressing his feelings openly is the opposite of the dissimulation practised—and only revealed to us by Shakespeare's dramatic technique of separate presentation—by the tribunes, the patricians, Aufidius and his conspirators. In all these juxtapositions Coriolanus' beliefs and actions are evaluated by Shakespeare as being superior to those of the people who surround and manipulate him.

It will be obvious by now that I take Coriolanus to be a true tragic hero. Yet that concept has acquired some unfortunate connotations in modern times, such as the idea that a hero must command our total approval. None of Shakespeare's tragic heroes would meet that requirement. If we think for a moment of Lear, Antony, Othello, Macbeth, Timon, Hamlet, then we will recall many instances where they behave with arrogance, stupidity, pride, jealousy, evil, malice. All have faults, yet we care for them all. What matters is that they should also have appreciable human values, should offer a way of living that we regard as precious, something that we would want to see preserved and not destroyed. In Coriolanus we admire his qualities of honesty, integrity, loyalty, self-sacrifice, love, tenderness, and respect—we admire them all the more since no one else in the play possesses them (though Cominius and Menenius on the public side, Virgilia on the private, do embody some of his values). The sharpness of the contrast which Shakespeare draws between him and his society derives much of its force from Coriolanus' extreme innocence. As Menenius says,

> Consider this: he hath been bred i'th'wars
> Since a'could draw a sword, and is ill schooled   (III.i.318f)

not only in 'bolted language'—fine talking—but in the whole nature of politics and social friction. Where he fails, then, is in the ability to recognize evil, to see how human beings 'have designs' on him. I recall Milton's phrase (in *Areopagitica*) for the dangers of anyone being 'a youngling in the contemplation of evil', or Bacon's insistence, discussing the 'impostures and vices of every profession', that the serious discussion of fraud should be considered 'among the best fortifications for honesty and virtue':

> For as the fable goes of the basilisk, that if he sees you first, you die for it, but if you see him first, he dies; so is it with deceits, impostures,

and evil arts, which, if they be first espied, they lose their life, but if they prevent [come first] they endanger; so that we are much beholden to Machiavelli and other writers of that class, who openly and unfeignedly declare or describe what men do, and not what they ought to do. For it is not possible to join the wisdom of the serpent with the innocence of the dove, except men be perfectly acquainted with the nature of evil itself; for without this, virtue is open and unfenced; nay, a virtuous and honest man can do no good upon those that are wicked, to correct and reclaim them, without first exploring all the depths and recesses of their malice. (*De Augmentis Scientiarum*, VII, i; trans. Spedding, V, 17)

Coriolanus' education has been misplanned: he ought to have been reading Bacon's *Essays* and Machiavelli's *Prince*. For he does possess much of 'the innocence of the dove' in politics, his virtue is entirely 'open and unfenced', he has no means either of defending himself or of correcting 'those that are wicked'. All that he can do, once he has seen the basilisk, is to exclaim in outrage, and attack it. But that is already too late.

Bacon's ethical dichotomy also applies to Coriolanus, who is to be aligned with the idealist position of 'what men ought to do', and only gradually discovers the gap between that and what they actually do. Yet—to pose a purely hypothetical question—would we wish him otherwise? If he had 'the wisdom of the serpent' wouldn't that totally transform his character? All his spontaneity and immediacy of feeling, whether anger or tenderness, his integrity, his noble trust and loyalty to others, all these would be replaced by self-control, the concealment and dissimulation of feelings, the careful calculation of personal advantage before acting. He would end up like Cominius or Aufidius. He might be the more successful general, of course, but the dichotomy that Shakespeare offers us is between his deficiencies as a political soldier and his strengths as a human being. I would rather have his integrity and innocence, however easily 'put upon', than all the calculation and political 'skill' in Rome or Corioli. In my support I cite a curiously apt passage in *War and Peace*. Prince Andrew Volkonski, observing a heated dispute between some generals, reflects that the so-called 'virtues' of a general are in fact such qualities as stupidity or absent-mindedness:

Not only does a good army commander not need any special qualities, on the contrary he needs the absence of the highest and best human attributes—love, poetry, tenderness, and philosophic inquiring doubt. He should be limited, firmly convinced that what he is doing is very important (otherwise he will not have sufficient patience), and only then will he be a brave leader. God forbid that he should be humane, should love, or pity, or think of what is just and unjust. (Bk 9, ch.11; trans. L. and A. Maude, 3 vols (London, 1939), Vol. 2, p. 308)

Tolstoy's irony resembles Shakespeare's : in some human activities it is better to fail than to succeed.

Bibliography

The text of the play used throughout is that edited by J. Dover Wilson (Cambridge, 1960). Three paperback editions, each useful in its own way, are by R. Brower (Signet), Harry Levin (Pelican), and G. R. Hibbard (New Penguin). The sources are best studied in Geoffrey Bullough's edition of the *Narrative and Dramatic Sources of Shakespeare, Volume V. The Roman Plays: Julius Caesar, Antony and Cleopatra, Coriolanus* (London, 1964). A useful survey of modern criticism is given by Maurice Charney in *Shakespeare. Select Bibliographical Guides*, ed. Stanley Wells (London, 1973), pp. 216ff.

Other books and articles referred to here are listed alphabetically. Items which support the interpretation of the play argued here are marked with an asterisk.

Bradley, A. C., '*Coriolanus*', British Academy Shakespeare Lecture 1912, reprinted in *Studies in Shakespeare*, ed. Peter Alexander (London, 1964).

*Browning, I. R., '*Coriolanus*: Boy of tears', *Essays in Criticism*, 5 (1955).

Burke, K., '*Coriolanus* and the Delights of Faction', *Hudson Review*, 19 (1966); reprinted in *Language as Symbolic Action* (Berkeley and Los Angeles, 1966).

Campbell, O. J., *Shakespeare's Satire* (New York and London, 1943).

Charney, M., *Shakespeare's Roman Plays: The Function of Imagery in the Drama* (Cambridge, Mass., 1961).

Dennis, J., *An Essay upon the Genius and Writings of Shakespeare*, in *Shakespeare. The Critical Heritage. Volume 2: 1693–1733*, ed. Brian Vickers (London, 1974).

Eliot, T. S., 'Hamlet and His Problems', (1919), in *Selected Essays* (London, 1932; reprinted 1961).

*Ellis-Fermor, Una, '*Coriolanus*', in *Shakespeare the Dramatist*, ed. K. Muir (London, 1961).

Enright, D. J., '*Coriolanus*: Tragedy or Debate', *Essays in Criticism*, 4 (1954); reprinted in *The Apothecary's Shop* (London, 1957).

Gordon, D. J., 'Name and Fame: Shakespeare's Coriolanus', in *Papers Mainly Shakespearian*, ed. G. I. Duthie (Edinburgh and London, 1964).

*Harding, D. W., 'Women's Fantasy of Manhood: A Shakespearian Theme', *Shakespeare Quarterly*, 20 (1969).

*Heuer, H., 'From Plutarch to Shakespeare: A study of *Coriolanus*', *Shakespeare Survey*, 10 (1957).

Knight, G. W., *The Imperial Theme* (London, 1931).

Lewis, Wyndham, *The Lion and the Fox* (London, 1927).

Muir, K., 'Shakespeare and the Tragic Pattern', British Academy Shakespeare Lecture, 1958: *Proceedings of the British Academy*, 44 (1959).

Palmer, J., *Political Characters of Shakespeare* (London, 1945).

Spencer, T. J. B., 'Shakespeare and the Elizabethan Romans', *Shakespeare Survey*, 10 (1957).

Traversi, D. A., *An Approach to Shakespeare* (London, 1957).

*Vickers, B. W., *The Artistry of Shakespeare's Prose* (London, 1968).

*Waith, E. M., *The Herculean Hero* (London, 1962).

Index

Stockton - Billingham
LIBRARY
Technical College